ZERO DAY MINDSET

Outsmarting Hackers Before They Strike

Ogochukwu Susan Ndibe

Published In Nigeria by:
Plexity Digital

CONTENTS

PREFACE

The story of cybersecurity is not a technical story alone. It is a human story, an evolving tale of ingenuity, trust, betrayal, and resilience. As I write these words, I am conscious of the fact that the battlefield of the digital world does not wait for anyone to catch up. Hackers are relentless in their pursuit of vulnerabilities and defenders must be even more relentless in outsmarting them. This book emerges from years of watching that race, analyzing the patterns, and understanding that the only way to truly stand ahead is to cultivate what I call the Zero Day Mindset. For too long, security has been reactive. Companies patch after the breach, governments legislate after the crisis, and individuals change habits only after losing something precious. This reactive stance gives attackers the advantage. A single vulnerability becomes a door through which not just one hacker can walk, but an entire network of adversaries can exploit. The Zero Day Mindset is not just about fixing problems but anticipating them. It is about thinking like the enemy, questioning assumptions, and recognizing that security is not a static state but an active discipline of foresight. The world has entered an age where everything is connected. Cars are computers on wheels, homes are controlled by smart devices, healthcare depends on digital systems, and financial markets move with the invisible currents of networks. Every one of these connections creates an opportunity for innovation and an equal opportunity for exploitation. Hackers exploit speed, complexity, and human error. The Zero Day Mindset insists that defenders can do the same but with greater purpose and clarity. By adopting this mindset, leaders, technologists, and individuals can transform themselves from passive defenders into strategic thinkers capable of reducing risks before they materialize. This book is not a technical manual, though it speaks the language of security. It is not a collection of fear-driven statistics, though it acknowledges the gravity of the threats. Instead, it is a call to think differently, to shift from the illusion of safety to the discipline of anticipation. I wrote it because I believe we cannot afford to continue approaching security as an afterthought. The mindset we cultivate determines whether we remain one step behind or one step ahead. As you move through the chapters, you will notice that the narrative builds toward a vision of empowerment. The goal is not only to understand cyber threats but to internalize a way of thinking that will remain relevant regardless of how technologies evolve. The attackers will always innovate, but so can you. The Zero Day Mindset ensures that innovation is not merely about creating new technologies but about protecting the trust that society places in them.

This book is written for leaders who must make decisions that impact entire organizations, for technologists who must design systems capable of resisting adversaries, and for individuals who want to navigate the digital age without being paralyzed by fear. It is written for anyone who believes that security is not a luxury but a necessity for survival and growth. I hope that, as you read, you find yourself not only informed but transformed. May you adopt a posture of vigilance that is proactive rather than reactive, strategic rather than panicked, confident rather than complacent. The Zero Day Mindset is not a theory to be admired but a discipline to be lived. If you embrace it, you will no longer be surprised by the moves of hackers because you will already be thinking ahead of them. That is the essence of outsmarting attackers before they strike.

FOREWORD

There are moments in history when society must pause and reimagine how it thinks about security. The invention of locks and keys changed the way we protected property. The rise of policing changed how communities organized against crime. The emergence of firewalls and antivirus software changed how computers defended against early digital threats. But today we are at the threshold of a new frontier where the old models of security no longer suffice. Hackers evolve faster than regulations, faster than businesses, faster than ordinary awareness. In this landscape, the Zero Day Mindset is not just timely, it is essential. I first encountered the author's work years ago in conversations about the failures of reactive cybersecurity. While the industry spoke in terms of patches, compliance checklists, and risk assessments, the argument was clear: all of this was not enough. Attackers thrive on surprise and defenders who wait for incidents are already defeated. What struck me then and continues to resonate now is the conviction that cybersecurity is not purely technical but fundamentally psychological. It is about how we perceive risk, how we anticipate moves, and how we cultivate habits of thought that deny adversaries the easy victories they seek. Reading this book, you will find no comfort in the idea that technology alone can save us. Instead, you will be challenged to rethink your own assumptions. You will be encouraged to put yourself in the shoes of attackers, to recognize the blind spots you have ignored, and to see security not as a set of products but as a living discipline that begins in the mind. This is not easy reading in the sense of giving quick solutions. It is demanding because it requires you to shift perspective. But therein lies its power. The Zero Day Mindset outlined here is more than strategy. It is philosophy translated into practice. It forces us to confront the uncomfortable truth that attackers will always be among us, probing, testing, and exploiting. Yet it also empowers us with the realization that by adopting a mindset of anticipation, we strip them of their advantage. When you think ahead, when you build resilience not just into systems but into culture, you create an environment where breaches are harder, risks are minimized, and trust is preserved. I believe this book belongs in the hands of every leader navigating the digital age, every professional tasked with defending critical systems, and every individual who refuses to be a passive victim of cyber threats. It is not just a guide for today's world but a blueprint for tomorrow. Reading it is like being invited into a higher level of thinking, one that sees beyond the noise of technical jargon into the core principle of security: foresight. The greatest contribution of this work is that it gives us language and framework for a reality many feel but cannot articulate. We all sense the fragility of our digital lives. We all know the anxiety of breaches and scams. But here we are given a structured way to not only understand those threats but to prepare for them. That is why this book matters. That is why the Zero Day Mindset is not optional but vital. As you read, prepare yourself for transformation. This is not a passive experience. It is a call to shift how you think, how you act, and how you lead in a world where hackers never sleep. And if you accept that call, you will walk away with more than knowledge. You will walk away with the clarity and confidence to outsmart adversaries before they strike.

INTRODUCTION

The digital world is a paradox of progress and peril. Every innovation that brings convenience also brings new opportunities for exploitation. Every connection that links us together creates a pathway for intrusion. Every line of code that powers our modern lives contains the possibility of vulnerability. In this paradox lies the urgency of rethinking how we approach security. The reality is that most of us are already targets, whether we know it or not. Hackers do not need to know your name to find value in your data. They do not need to hate your organization to exploit its weaknesses. They are opportunists in a digital environment that is more open than it appears. For decades, the dominant model of cybersecurity has been defensive and reactive. We wait for an incident, we investigate, and then we apply patches. The cycle continues endlessly and with each new attack, defenders scramble to catch up. This approach is unsustainable. In a world where threats evolve daily and adversaries think creatively, reacting after the fact is the equivalent of locking the door after the intruder has already left with your possessions. What is needed is not simply better locks or faster alarms, but a new mindset altogether. The Zero Day Mindset represents this shift. It is the ability to think like attackers while defending against them. It is the practice of anticipating not just the vulnerabilities you already know but the ones you have not yet discovered. It is the recognition that the battle is not only fought in lines of code but in habits of thought. Hackers succeed because they exploit blind spots. They thrive on assumptions. They understand that most defenders are constrained by routine thinking. To outsmart them, defenders must break free from those same constraints. This introduction is not an invitation to fear. Fear immobilizes and blinds. What is needed is clarity and courage. The Zero Day Mindset is not built on panic but on preparation. It equips you to ask better questions. Where would I attack if I were the adversary? What blind spots am I ignoring? How do I design systems and cultures that are resilient not only against known threats but against the unknown? These questions transform security from a burden into a discipline of foresight. You will discover in this book that adopting the Zero Day Mindset requires a blend of technical literacy and psychological awareness. It is not enough to understand encryption or firewalls. You must also understand how humans behave under pressure, how trust is manipulated, how complacency creeps into even the best teams. Hackers exploit not just machines but people. To outsmart them, you must address both. Throughout the chapters, we will explore how anticipation beats reaction, how resilience is built before crises, and how individuals and organizations can make security a living practice rather than a checklist. You will see examples from across industries, stories of failures that could have been prevented, and strategies that turn vulnerabilities into opportunities for strength. Each lesson reinforces the central truth: the battle is won not in the moment of attack but in the mindset, you cultivate before the attack comes. The Zero Day Mindset is not a guarantee that you will never face threats. No guarantee exists. Instead, it is the discipline of reducing risks, limiting damage, and maintaining trust even in a hostile environment. It is the difference between being a constant victim and being an active defender. It is the choice to think ahead rather than wait helplessly. As you begin this journey, remember that security is not a destination. It is a living, breathing practice. The adversaries will not stop evolving, but neither must you. With the Zero Day Mindset, you will find yourself not merely surviving in the digital age but thriving in it, confident in your ability to outthink, outmaneuver, and outlast those who would exploit your vulnerabilities. That is the mindset of tomorrow's defender. That is the mindset this book invites you to adopt today.

The digital world is no longer an optional part of our lives. It is the foundation on which nearly every interaction, transaction, and decision now rests. From the way we work to the way we travel, from the systems that power our cities to the devices we carry in our pockets, the infrastructure of the modern world is digital at its core. Yet beneath this seamless flow of connectivity lies a constant reality that most people prefer not to confront. Every connection is also an exposure, every advancement is also a vulnerability, and every system is only as strong as its weakest point. This is not a statement of pessimism but of truth, and until we confront it directly, we will always remain one step behind those who exploit it. The conventional wisdom of security has long relied on reaction. Something breaks, and we fix it. A breach occurs, and we investigate. A new exploit emerges, and we release a patch. The entire cycle depends on events happening before solutions are implemented. This is the problem. Hackers do not play by the rules of reaction. They play by the rules of anticipation. They live in the mindset of tomorrow, searching not for what is already broken but for what could be broken. They are rewarded for imagination, for probing where no one has yet looked, for turning innovation itself into a weapon. Against such adversaries, waiting for an attack before responding is not only ineffective but reckless. This is why the concept of a Zero Day vulnerability has always struck a chord with those who understand security at its core. A Zero Day is not merely a flaw in a piece of code. It is a metaphor for the unseen, the unknown, the unprepared. It represents the gap between what defenders believe to be secure and what attackers already know to be insecure. It is the embodiment of surprise. To live with a Zero Day Mindset is to accept that surprise as inevitable and to prepare for it not with fear but with foresight. It is to build systems, strategies, and cultures that anticipate threats before they materialize, rather than scrambling once they arrive. The average person imagines a hacker as a figure in the shadows, a hooded silhouette typing lines of code in isolation. The reality is both simpler and more complex. Hackers are opportunists. They may be lone actors driven by curiosity or malice. They may be organized groups funded by states or corporations. They may be automated systems that probe millions of targets at once. What unites them is their mindset. They ask questions defenders often fail to ask. Where is the blind spot? What assumption is everyone making that I can exploit? What small oversight opens the door to larger gain? That mindset is not inherently malicious. In fact, it is the same mindset that drives innovation. The difference is in how it is applied. The Zero Day Mindset is about reclaiming that way of thinking and turning it toward defense. Imagine if organizations trained their teams to anticipate vulnerabilities before attackers found them. Imagine if individuals approached their digital lives not with paranoia but with informed awareness. Imagine if leaders stopped treating security as an expense and began treating it as a culture. This is not an impossible vision. It requires no extraordinary genius. What it requires is a shift in how we perceive security itself. Most people consider security as a barrier, something external that protects them from threats. In reality, security is more like oxygen. It is invisible, often taken for granted, but essential for survival. You rarely think about it until it is gone. The Zero Day Mindset insists that security must become as natural and habitual as breathing. It should not be a checklist item that teams complete to satisfy regulations. It should not be an afterthought when a product is already designed. It should not be the responsibility of one department while the rest of the organization moves forward unchecked. Security must be embedded into every decision, every design, every assumption. When it becomes part of the culture, it no longer feels like a barrier. It feels like resilience. The danger of remaining reactive is not only technical but psychological. Organizations that respond only after incidents often develop a culture of blame. Employees fear admitting mistakes. Teams become siloed. Leaders focus more on damage control than on prevention. This culture feeds complacency and fear, both of which are fertile ground for attackers. By contrast, organizations that embrace the Zero Day Mindset build cultures of openness and anticipation. Mistakes are examined before they escalate. Weaknesses are acknowledged as opportunities for improvement. People are encouraged to think critically about how systems could fail and how to strengthen them. The result is not paranoia but confidence. Consider the scale of what is at stake. Hospitals now depend on digital infrastructure for life-saving equipment. Airlines depend on software for navigation and safety. Financial institutions move trillions in invisible exchanges every second. Governments manage defense, power grids, and transportation through digital systems. A single oversight in any of these arenas is not just a technical issue. It is a matter of life, trust, and stability. Yet the same reality extends to individuals. A stolen identity can destroy years of financial stability. A breached account can compromise both personal and professional relationships. A targeted scam can leave lasting psychological scars. The stakes are universal, from the largest institutions to the smallest households. The Zero Day Mindset is not about guaranteeing that nothing will ever go wrong. Perfection is unattainable. It is about ensuring that when something does go wrong, the impact is minimized, recovery is swift, and trust is preserved. It is about cultivating foresight so that surprises are fewer, risks are smaller, and vulnerabilities are less exploitable. It is about making sure that you are no longer caught in the endless cycle of reaction but are instead living in a state of readiness. Adopting this mindset begins with asking the right questions. If I were an attacker, how would I exploit this system? If I were looking for the easiest point of entry, where would it be? What assumptions am I making that a hacker would challenge? These questions are simple but powerful. They force us to step outside our habits and view our environments through the lens of potential exploitation. They reveal blind spots before adversaries do. They shift the balance of power away from attackers and back toward defenders. The introduction you are now reading is not meant to comfort you into thinking that technology alone can solve the problem. It is meant to awaken you to the reality that technology without mindset is hollow. Firewalls can be bypassed. Encryption can be broken. Software can be patched too late. But a mindset of anticipation, of foresight, of preparation cannot be so easily defeated. It transforms not only how systems are built but how people think about them. It builds resilience not as an add-on but as a foundation. As we proceed through this book, we will examine the psychological, cultural, and technical dimensions of the Zero Day Mindset. We will explore real-world examples where failures of foresight led to catastrophic breaches and where proactive thinking could have prevented them. We will analyze strategies that individuals and organizations can adopt to reduce risk and increase resilience. Most importantly, we will emphasize that this is not just about hackers and systems but about human beings, their decisions, and the trust they hold in the digital age. The journey ahead is both challenging and empowering. It demands that you rethink what you know about security, question your assumptions, and embrace discomfort as the beginning of wisdom. It will ask you to see yourself not as a passive defender waiting for the next wave of attacks but as an active strategist capable of thinking ahead. If you accept that invitation, you will find yourself in possession of something far more powerful than any tool or software. You will have a mindset that keeps you ahead, a mindset that strips attackers of their advantage, a mindset that turns surprise into preparedness. That is the Zero Day Mindset. That is the way forward in a world where digital threats are constant and evolving.

CHAPTER 1

The Illusion of Safety in a Connected World

Human beings have always sought comfort in the idea of safety. From the walls of ancient cities to the locks on modern doors, we build protections that make us feel secure even if they are not impenetrable. The digital world has created its own version of this comfort. Firewalls, passwords, antivirus software, and multi-factor authentication create an environment where users feel insulated from danger. The sense of safety is reassuring, yet it is fragile. Beneath the surface, attackers search for cracks, and when they find them, the illusion of safety dissolves instantly. The psychology of false security is one of the greatest vulnerabilities in the digital age. People assume that once a product is released, it must be safe. They believe that because their system shows a lock icon or their device updates regularly, they are protected. This belief creates complacency. Attackers exploit that complacency with precision. They know that the easiest targets are not always the least protected but the most overconfident. They understand that security measures are often treated as boxes to be checked rather than living practices to be maintained.

Organizations also fall prey to the illusion of safety. A company invests heavily in a security product, then assumes it is shielded from danger. Employees are trained once, and the training is never repeated. Policies are written but rarely updated. Systems are monitored but only for known threats. In reality, the digital battlefield changes daily. What was secure yesterday may be vulnerable today. To believe otherwise is to live in denial, and denial is a hacker's greatest ally. The illusion of safety extends beyond individuals and organizations. Nations depend on critical infrastructures that are connected to digital systems. Power grids, transportation networks, and healthcare services all rely on software that is assumed to be reliable. Yet history shows that assumptions of reliability often precede moments of crisis. The interconnectedness that powers progress also multiplies risks. A single vulnerability can cascade across networks, magnifying its impact in ways that no one anticipated. When nations, corporations, and individuals embrace false comfort, they collectively create an environment where attackers thrive. The Zero Day Mindset begins with dismantling this illusion. It requires acknowledging that safety is not a fixed state but a dynamic effort. It requires vigilance that is proactive rather than reactive. It requires a willingness to question the comfort of routines, to test assumptions, and to prepare for the unseen. Only when the illusion is broken can genuine resilience begin.

The Hacker's Advantage

To understand why the illusion of safety is dangerous, one must also understand the nature of the hacker's advantage. Hackers do not play by the same rules as defenders. Defenders must secure every point of vulnerability while attackers need only find one. This imbalance creates a game where time favors the adversary. Every new technology, every new connection, every new update is an opportunity for exploitation. The defender sees progress. The attacker sees possibility. The hacker's advantage is not only technical but psychological. Hackers approach systems with curiosity unburdened by rules. They ask questions that defenders rarely consider. What assumption has been made that I can undermine? What shortcut has been taken that I can exploit? What blind spot exists because no one dared to imagine it? This freedom of thought gives them creativity that defenders often lack. Bureaucracy, regulation, and habit constrain defenders, while hackers are limited only by imagination. Another dimension of their advantage lies in their community. Hackers are not isolated figures in the shadows. They are connected to networks of knowledge sharing, marketplaces of exploits, and forums where information circulates freely. When one discovers a vulnerability, others learn from it. When one tool is created, it spreads rapidly. Defenders, by contrast, often work in silos.

Information about breaches is withheld out of fear of reputation damage. Lessons learned are not always shared across industries. This secrecy perpetuates weakness. Hackers learn collectively, defenders learn individually. The result is an imbalance of knowledge that strengthens attackers further. Hackers also thrive on time. A vulnerability discovered today may not be exploited immediately. Instead, it may be sold, stockpiled, or quietly observed until the perfect moment. This patience ensures maximum impact. Defenders, however, are often trapped in cycles of urgency, reacting to what has already happened rather than preparing for what could happen. The hacker's advantage is in choosing the time of battle while defenders are caught by surprise. The Zero Day Mindset seeks to level this imbalance by reclaiming curiosity, community, and time. Defenders must learn to think with the same imagination as attackers, to build networks of shared knowledge, and to prepare strategies before vulnerabilities are exploited. By shifting the mindset, the advantage no longer rests solely with the hacker. It becomes a contest not of surprise but of foresight, not of imbalance but of resilience.

The Path to Awareness

Breaking the illusion of safety and understanding the hacker's advantage leads naturally to the next step, which is awareness. Awareness is not mere knowledge of threats. It is a disciplined recognition of how those threats intersect with our lives, systems, and decisions. It is the ability to see beyond the surface of convenience into the underlying structures of vulnerability. Without awareness, security becomes nothing more than a checklist. With awareness, it becomes a way of thinking that permeates every action. Awareness begins with the individual. Every person who interacts with technology is part of the security ecosystem. A careless click, a weak password, or an unverified link can create openings that ripple far beyond the individual. Awareness requires acknowledging responsibility. It means recognizing that security is not the job of specialists alone but the duty of everyone who participates in the digital age. When individuals adopt habits of vigilance, the collective environment becomes harder to exploit. For organizations, awareness must be cultural rather than procedural. Policies cannot exist only on paper. They must live in the daily practices of employees. Awareness means training is not a one-time event but a continuous process. It means leaders model vigilance rather than delegating it. It means systems are evaluated not only for functionality but for resilience. Awareness is the difference between treating security as a burden and embracing it as part of organizational identity. On a societal level, awareness requires transparency and education. Too often, breaches are hidden, lessons are buried, and the public is left uninformed. This secrecy benefits attackers, who thrive in the shadows of ignorance. Awareness at the societal level means governments, institutions, and industries must communicate openly about risks, share information across boundaries, and invest in education that equips citizens with the skills to navigate digital threats. A society that understands security is far less vulnerable than one that pretends it does not need to. The Zero Day Mindset is the culmination of this awareness. It is the recognition that threats are constant, that attackers are imaginative, and that safety is not given but earned through vigilance. It transforms security from an afterthought into a foundation. It replaces denial with readiness. It turns fear into strategy. Awareness does not eliminate risk, but it ensures that risks are confronted with clarity rather than surprise. The journey of this book begins here, with the recognition that the greatest danger is not the hacker outside but the complacency within. The illusion of safety blinds us. The hacker's advantage exploits us. Awareness empowers us. To adopt the Zero Day Mindset is to move beyond comfort into clarity, beyond reaction into preparation, beyond illusion into resilience. It is to step into a world where you no longer wait for threats to reveal themselves but where you anticipate them, adapt to them, and outsmart them before they strike.

CHAPTER 2

The Anatomy of a Breach

Every breach begins with an entry point and while people often imagine this as a dramatic moment where a hacker forcefully breaks into a system the truth is that most breaches begin quietly in places few are considered worth guarding. Entry points are often invisible because they blend into the everyday rhythm of digital life. An email inbox becomes a doorway when a link is clicked without suspicion. A forgotten software update becomes a welcome mat when a known vulnerability is left unpatched. A misplaced device becomes a set of keys handed to an intruder. The genius of attackers lies in recognizing that defenders cannot guard everything equally and so they seek out the weakest links where defenses are thinnest and attention is minimal. What makes these entry points even more dangerous is the human tendency to underestimate them. Employees assume that a simple password is harmless if only used for minor accounts, yet attackers know that people often reuse credentials across multiple platforms. What begins as access to an insignificant account can evolve into entry into sensitive systems. The illusion of separation between personal and professional accounts further weakens defenses as attackers exploit overlaps to escalate access. Invisible entry points also exist in supply chains where third party vendors connect their systems to larger organizations. An attacker who cannot penetrate a major corporation directly may instead target its smaller partners with weaker protections and then use that connection as a pathway into the larger target. History is filled with examples of breaches where the weakest link was not the company itself but the vendor providing services. These invisible entries highlight a critical truth which is that security is only as strong as the least protected connection. Attackers understand this reality intuitively and defenders must learn to embrace the same perspective. The Zero Day Mindset means assuming that every point of connection, every forgotten account, every unmonitored device and every vendor relationship is a potential doorway for intrusion. It means acknowledging that no detail is too small to be exploited and that vigilance must extend into the corners of digital ecosystems that are often ignored. Only when defenders accept the ubiquity of these entry points can they begin to build strategies that anticipate rather than react to breaches.

The Life Cycle of an Attack

Once an entry point is exploited the breach follows a life cycle that unfolds in stages often invisible until damage is already done. Attackers rarely strike in a single chaotic burst. Instead, they move with patience, methodical precision and an understanding that time is their ally. The first stage is infiltration where the attacker gains initial access often through compromised credentials phishing emails or unpatched vulnerabilities. At this point defenders might still have a chance to detect anomalies but because the intrusion is subtle it often goes unnoticed. The attacker then moves into reconnaissance quietly exploring the system mapping its structure and identifying valuable assets. They search for sensitive data, administrative privileges, and pathways that lead deeper into the environment. This stage can last days, weeks or even months and it is during this period that the attacker learns how to blend in with normal activity to avoid detection. Once reconnaissance provides clarity the attacker advances to escalation where they seek higher levels of access. This may involve privilege escalation attacks where limited accounts are transformed into powerful ones or lateral movement where the attacker moves across networks to expand control. Each escalation deepens the attacker's foothold making removal more difficult. The next stage is exploitation where the attacker begins extracting value whether through data theft, financial fraud disruption of services or preparation for ransom ware deployment. By this stage the breach often becomes visible to defenders but by then the damage is already significant. The final stage is persistence where the attacker builds backdoors ensuring future access even if initial entry points are discovered and closed. This life cycle demonstrates that breaches are not random events but carefully orchestrated campaigns. Attackers do not merely want to enter systems they want to live inside them undetected for as long as possible. Defenders who imagine breaches as sudden explosions misunderstand the reality. The true danger lies in the slow patient buildup that remains hidden until too late. The Zero Day Mindset requires defenders to invert their perspective. Rather than waiting for the exploitation stage to sound alarms they must focus on early detection during infiltration and reconnaissance. This means monitoring unusual patterns of behavior no matter how subtle, questioning anomalies that might otherwise be dismissed, and investing in proactive threat hunting rather than passive monitoring. Recognizing the life cycle of an attack shifts defense from reaction to anticipation and transforms security from a waiting game into a contest of foresight.

The Human Factor Behind Every Breach

While the technical details of entry points and attack life cycles are essential the ultimate reality is that behind every breach lies a human factor. Technology provides the tools, but it is human decisions that open the doors. Attackers exploit not just machines but the psychology habits and mistakes of people. Phishing emails succeed because curiosity and trust override caution. Weak passwords exist because convenience is chosen over discipline. Updates are ignored because routine takes precedence over vigilance. Even highly secure organizations are vulnerable if their employees do not embrace security as part of their identity. The human factor extends beyond employees to executives whose decisions shape organizational priorities. Leaders who undervalue cybersecurity leave their organizations exposed by underfunding defenses, treating security as a compliance requirement rather than a strategic necessity, or assuming that investment in a single technology will eliminate risk. Attackers understand this dynamic, and they thrive on it. They know that organizations driven by speed and efficiency will often cut corners on security and they design their strategies accordingly. The human factor is also evident in attackers themselves. Their motivations vary from financial gain to political agendas to sheer curiosity and these motivations shape the nature of the breaches they conduct. Some attackers are opportunists exploiting vulnerabilities wherever they find them while others are targeted adversaries with patience and long term strategies. Understanding the human factor on both sides of the equation is essential for building effective defenses. The Zero Day Mindset recognizes that no technology can fully compensate for human negligence or misjudgment. Training must go beyond checklists to instill a culture where security is second nature. Employees must be empowered not just instructed, leaders must model vigilance not just demand it, and organizations must treat every human interaction with technology as a potential point of strength or weakness. At the same time defenders must understand the mindset of attackers to anticipate their moves. By studying how attackers think, what motivates them and how they exploit human behavior, defenders can build strategies that not only close technical gaps but also address psychological ones. The greatest breach is not simply a matter of code but of human choice and the Zero Day Mindset turns that choice into an advantage by fostering awareness discipline and foresight at every level.

CHAPTER 3

Curiosity as a Weapon

To understand how hackers outmaneuver defenders one must first grasp the psychology that drives them because at the heart of every attack lies curiosity turned into a weapon. Hackers are not bound by the same assumptions as ordinary users and they do not see systems as static tools meant to be used only in prescribed ways. Instead, they see them as puzzles waiting to be taken apart and reassembled, challenges begging to be overcome, and opportunities hidden behind layers of complexity. Curiosity is the spark that ignites their exploration. Where most people stop at what is functional hackers dig into what is possible. If a button leads to one action, they ask what happens if it is pressed differently. If code is meant to execute one task they question whether it can be rewritten to perform another. This questioning mindset is what allows them to see cracks invisible to those who trust systems as they are. Curiosity on its own might seem harmless yet in the hands of hackers it becomes a weapon because they pair it with persistence and technical skill. They do not stop when the first barrier resists. Instead, resistance excites them because it signals hidden value. Every error message becomes a clue. Every denied request becomes an invitation. Every system restriction becomes a puzzle piece. What frustrates defenders energizes attackers. This transformation of obstacles into fuel makes their curiosity uniquely dangerous. Defenders often underestimate curiosity because they believe that technology is only as powerful as its documented capabilities. They assume that software functions according to the rules written in manuals or described by vendors. Hackers however thrive in the undocumented spaces where no rulebook exists. They explore not what was intended but what is possible, and they uncover ways of bending systems that their creators never imagined. When curiosity is combined with a sense of play it becomes even more dangerous. Many hackers treat digital systems as playgrounds where experimentation carries no immediate consequence, and this playful mindset makes them fearless in exploration. While defenders worry about stability uptime and compliance hackers chase the thrill of discovery. The Zero Day Mindset requires defenders to cultivate a similar form of curiosity but redirected toward protection rather than exploitation. It means asking what assumptions underlie every system, what could go wrong if those assumptions fail, what might an attacker see that we do not. Without curiosity defenders remain reactive but with it they anticipate the unknown. Curiosity becomes a shield rather than a weapon and the game begins to shift.

Motivation Beyond Money

While curiosity explains how hackers think it does not fully explain why they act. Motivation is the second pillar of the hacker's mind, and it extends far beyond the pursuit of money. Certainly, financial gain fuels many breaches, particularly in the form of ransomware attacks, credit card theft, or cryptocurrency fraud, yet reducing hacker motivation to greed alone misses the broader landscape. Some hackers are motivated by ideology, believing they are fighting for a political cause or exposing corruption. Hacktivist groups operate with agendas that blur the line between protest and crime. They breach systems not to enrich themselves but to send a message, embarrass a target, or advance a worldview. For defenders this type of motivation is dangerous because it is unpredictable. Financially driven attackers may withdraw when profit is no longer feasible but ideologically driven ones persist even when odds are stacked against them. Another form of motivation comes from status within hacker communities. Just as athletes compete for recognition hackers compete for credibility. Discovering a new vulnerability, publishing an exploit or successfully breaching a high profile target elevates one's reputation within underground circles. This pursuit of respect and notoriety transforms hacking into a cultural phenomenon where recognition becomes a currency more valuable than money itself. In such cases defenders must understand that their systems are not simply functional assets but trophies that attackers may covet. Ego also plays a role in motivation. Some hackers act from a desire to prove superiority, to challenge authority, or to outwit experts. The act of breaching a system becomes a demonstration of intellect. The harder the target the greater the satisfaction in overcoming it. This mindset creates a paradox for defenders because stronger security often attracts more determined attackers who view it as a worthy test. The Zero Day Mindset recognizes that motivation is as diverse as the individuals who carry it. Financial gain ideology status ego curiosity boredom or even revenge can all drive hackers into action. What unites them is not the specific reward but the relentless drive to achieve it despite obstacles. Understanding motivation allows defenders to predict not only how attacks may occur but why certain targets are chosen. It highlights that cybersecurity is not solely a technological contest but a human one rooted in desires, beliefs, and rivalries. When defenders fail to grasp these deeper motivations, they risk fighting the wrong battles and leaving themselves exposed to threats they did not anticipate. By studying motivation, they not only prepare for the attacks of today but also for the evolving threats of tomorrow.

Thinking Like the Adversary

If curiosity reveals how hackers explore, and motivation explains why they persist then the final dimension of the hacker's mind is the ability to think differently from defenders. Attackers do not see boundaries in the same way. They operate outside regulations and ethical limits, granting them a freedom of imagination that defenders often lack. To think like an adversary means to abandon assumptions of safety and to consider every possibility no matter how unlikely or uncomfortable. Hackers constantly ask what could be exploited if rules were ignored, what weakness would appear if someone acted without constraint, and what vulnerability might exist in places where no one bothers to look. This inversion of perspective is what makes them effective. For defenders the challenge is that traditional training rarely fosters adversarial thinking. Security programs focus on compliance, on meeting standards, and on implementing best practices. These measures are valuable, but they cultivate a mindset of following rules rather than challenging them. Attackers, however, are not bound by rules. They do not care if a company is certified compliant with a standard. They care only about the gap between compliance and reality. The Zero Day Mindset demands that defenders learn to adopt adversarial thinking not to exploit but to anticipate. It requires leaders and analysts to regularly ask themselves how I would attack this system if I wanted to cause maximum damage, where the points of trust that could be abused, and what blind spots exist because everyone assumes they are safe. By stepping into the mindset of an adversary defenders transform their strategy from static defense into dynamic anticipation. Thinking like an adversary also means embracing creativity. Attackers innovate constantly by chaining vulnerabilities together in ways no single defender anticipated. A minor misconfiguration in one system combined with a careless user action in another can produce a pathway to total compromise. Defenders who think narrowly miss these connections while attackers who think broadly exploit them. Creativity in defense means considering the interconnectedness of systems, the unpredictability of human behavior, and the persistence of adversaries. It means designing not only for what is expected but for what is possible. Another dimension of adversarial thinking is patience. Hackers often play the long game watching silently for weeks or months before acting. Defenders focused only on immediate alerts may overlook slow moving threats. To think like an adversary is to imagine not only sudden attacks but prolonged campaigns designed to exhaust attention and erode vigilance. The Zero Day Mindset therefore shifts defenders from short term reaction to long term anticipation. The ultimate lesson of thinking like the adversary is that security is not about building perfect walls but about staying a step ahead in imagination. Hackers will always search for new entry points, new methods, and new motivations. Defenders who wait to respond are already behind. Those who adopt the mindset of the adversary however reclaim initiative.

They turn security from a reactive shield into a proactive strategy, not merely resisting attacks but predicting and outsmarting them before they strike.

CHAPTER 4

The Business of Cybercrime

Cybercrime is no longer the work of isolated individuals tinkering in basements for thrill or rebellion but a vast economy operating in the shadows, structured, organized, and in many ways resembling legitimate industries. At its foundation lies a marketplace where stolen data, malicious software, and exploit kits are traded with the same efficiency as consumer goods on open platforms. Hackers who once had to build their own tools from scratch now purchase ready-made solutions, complete with customer support, user manuals, and updates. This commercialization of crime lowers the barrier of entry so that even those with minimal technical skill can participate in sophisticated attacks simply by buying services from more experienced actors. Credit card numbers, banking credentials, and medical records flow across underground forums as commodities with fluctuating prices determined by freshness, volume, and quality. Entire ecosystems exist to ensure supply chains are maintained. Data stolen in one breach may be packaged by another group, resold by a third, and monetized by a fourth, demonstrating how cybercrime has matured into a collaborative enterprise. Beyond data, access itself is sold as a product. Criminals offer remote entry into compromised systems, sometimes even advertising corporate networks as if they were real estate listings, complete with descriptions of what assets lie inside. The rise of ransomware as a service further illustrates this evolution, where operators create the malware, affiliates deploy it, and profits are shared much like franchise models. This professionalization brings efficiency and scalability that mirror legitimate businesses. There are even dispute resolution mechanisms within underground forums to handle conflicts between criminals, and reputational systems where sellers build trust among buyers by delivering on promises. The underground economy thrives because it adapts quickly. When law enforcement disrupts one marketplace another emerges within days. When payment methods become restricted, new cryptocurrencies or anonymizing techniques are adopted. This resilience demonstrates that cybercrime is not a chaotic mess but an organized system capable of withstanding pressure and reinventing itself continuously. For defenders and policymakers, the lesson is sobering. They are not facing lone individuals but an industry with its own incentives, resources, and innovation cycles. The Zero Day Mindset requires acknowledging that cybercrime is not peripheral but central to the global economy of the digital age, and only by understanding its inner workings can meaningful disruption occur.

The Corporate Victims

For businesses, the reality of cybercrime is not abstract but painfully concrete because corporations have become the primary targets and victims of this underground economy. What makes them attractive is the wealth of data they hold, the critical infrastructure they manage, and the financial resources they can be extorted for. Attackers understand that businesses will often pay to restore services, avoid publicity, or prevent regulatory scrutiny, making them ideal prey. Breaches rarely affect only a single department. Instead, they ripple across entire organizations, compromising customer trust, disrupting supply chains, and in severe cases threatening survival itself. The cost is not only financial but reputational. Customers who entrust personal information to a company expect that information to be safeguarded, and when it is exposed, the bond of trust fractures instantly. Restoring it can take years, if it is ever restored at all. For corporations the stakes are therefore existential. Attackers exploit this pressure deliberately. Ransomware operators often time their strikes to coincide with moments of high business dependency, such as product launches, financial reporting cycles, or peak shopping seasons, ensuring maximum leverage. They research their targets in advance, knowing who holds decision making power, what data is most critical, and how much the organization can afford to pay. These targeted campaigns demonstrate that cybercrime has evolved into precision operations tailored for maximum impact. Beyond immediate attacks corporations face long term consequences. Regulatory fines increase as governments impose stricter data protection laws. Investors lose confidence when breaches expose weaknesses in governance. Employees suffer anxiety, distraction, and lost productivity as internal systems are disrupted. The compounding nature of these effects means that a single breach can influence an organization's trajectory for years. Some never recover. Even large corporations with extensive resources are not immune. History has shown that the size of an organization does not equate to immunity but to greater visibility and higher stakes. Smaller businesses face different vulnerabilities. They may lack the resources to invest in robust defenses, making them easier targets, and yet they often act as entry points into larger organizations through partnerships and vendor relationships. In this way attackers exploit not only corporations directly but also the interconnected ecosystem in which they operate. The Zero Day Mindset challenges corporations to recognize that security is not a department but a culture, not a cost center but a survival strategy. Leaders must treat cybersecurity as integral to reputation, trust, and long term growth. To underestimate this is to invite catastrophe, for in the business of cybercrime corporations are not only targets but commodities, traded, exploited, and monetized within the underground economy.

Law Enforcement and the Global Challenge

Confronting cybercrime is not as simple as shutting down one group or arresting one individual because the problem transcends borders, legal systems, and traditional notions of jurisdiction. Law enforcement faces a global challenge where attackers can operate from one country, target victims in another, route traffic through several others, and receive payments in currencies that defy traceability. This borderless nature of cybercrime makes it uniquely difficult to police. Agencies in one nation may pursue criminals aggressively, but without cooperation from others the effort stalls. Extradition treaties are limited, legal frameworks differ, and some states even provide safe havens either by neglect or by deliberate strategy. In certain cases, governments themselves are implicated as sponsors of cyber activity, using criminal infrastructures to advance espionage or strategic objectives. This blurring of lines between state actors and criminal actors complicates responses further, for what begins as crime may merge into geopolitics. Law enforcement has made significant strides through international collaborations, joint task forces, and intelligence sharing platforms, but challenges remain immense. Criminals adapt quickly, exploiting bureaucratic delays and legal inconsistencies to stay ahead. Even when groups are disrupted, the vacuum is swiftly filled by others. Arrests rarely dismantle entire ecosystems, and prosecutions often lag far behind the speed at which new techniques and tools emerge. Beyond legal hurdles, technological barriers complicate enforcement. Encryption and anonymization make it difficult to track activities. Cryptocurrencies create financial trails that require specialized expertise to follow. Cloud infrastructures spread data across multiple jurisdictions, each with its own laws. These realities mean that even when law enforcement acts swiftly, the structural advantages remain with attackers. Yet hope lies in collaboration not only among nations but also between public and private sectors. Many of the insights into criminal operations come from corporations, researchers, and independent cybersecurity experts. When this knowledge is shared openly, law enforcement can act with greater precision. Partnerships have already led to takedowns of marketplaces, dismantling of botnets, and arrests of prominent actors, proving that coordinated efforts can make meaningful dents in the problem. Still, the Zero Day Mindset emphasizes that waiting for enforcement alone is insufficient. Organizations and individuals must assume responsibility for their own resilience, preparing as though the law will not arrive in time to prevent harm. Enforcement is necessary but not sufficient. The global challenge requires a mindset where protection begins at the individual and organizational level, scales upward into industries, and finally converges with law enforcement. Only then can the balance shift. Cybercrime will not vanish, but with foresight, cooperation, and a mindset of preparation, its impact can be contained.

CHAPTER 5

The Evolution of Threats in a Hyperconnected Era

The rise of the hyperconnected era has transformed not only the way individuals, businesses, and governments communicate but also the nature of threats that exist within this vast digital ecosystem. As connectivity has expanded, threats have grown more sophisticated, targeting every layer of technology and every weakness in human behavior. Unlike the early days of the internet when threats were limited to viruses that disrupted systems or worms that spread through floppy disks, the digital age has witnessed a shift toward highly advanced, adaptive, and persistent attacks that can cripple entire infrastructures. Cybercriminals no longer operate in isolation, many now work within highly organized groups with access to global resources, and even state actors participate in offensive cyber operations with motives that go beyond financial gain to include espionage, sabotage, and geopolitical influence. In this context, understanding the evolution of threats becomes essential to outsmarting hackers before they strike. The first noticeable transformation lies in the diversification of threat actors. Previously, hackers were often individuals seeking recognition or amusement, testing their skills by infiltrating vulnerable systems. Today, however, the threat landscape includes cybercriminal syndicates, hacktivists with ideological motivations, insider threats within organizations, and state-sponsored groups that leverage cutting-edge tools. Each category of attacker carries unique strategies and intentions, but all exploit the same reality: the dependence of modern society on digital infrastructure. The attacks of yesterday were nuisances, but the attacks of today carry real economic, political, and social consequences. The rise of ransomware, for instance, illustrates how cyber threats have shifted from destructive mischief to profitable ventures. Criminal groups now encrypt critical organizational data and demand payments in cryptocurrency, paralyzing hospitals, schools, and even government agencies. Beyond financial extortion, these attacks jeopardize public trust in essential institutions. Another dimension of evolution lies in the tools hackers use. The democratization of hacking through the dark web and underground forums has made powerful tools accessible to almost anyone. Malware kits, exploit frameworks, and phishing templates can be purchased cheaply, reducing the barrier to entry for cybercrime. Artificial intelligence and machine learning, once reserved for research labs, are now leveraged by attackers to automate reconnaissance, improve phishing campaigns with convincing personalization, and adapt malware in real time. This technological acceleration makes threats dynamic, constantly mutating to avoid detection. As defenders develop new tools to identify malicious activity, attackers respond by developing countermeasures, creating a perpetual cycle of adaptation. The globalization of threats further complicates the landscape. A cybercriminal in one part of the world can target victims thousands of miles away with minimal effort, exploiting the borderless nature of the internet. Coordinated attacks across jurisdictions challenge law enforcement, as cooperation between nations remains slow and inconsistent. Moreover, advanced persistent threats backed by nation states are designed to infiltrate systems quietly, often lying dormant for years while exfiltrating data or monitoring sensitive communications. Such threats are not easily mitigated because they blend into normal activity, making detection difficult. In this sense, the evolution of threats reflects not just the ingenuity of attackers but also the vulnerabilities inherent in interconnected systems that prioritize convenience and speed over security.

At the heart of this evolution is the human factor. Despite technological defenses, many successful attacks exploit human weaknesses such as poor password practices, susceptibility to social engineering, or lack of security awareness. Phishing remains one of the most effective methods of infiltration, not because systems are weak, but because humans are fallible.

Attackers understand this and exploit psychology, manipulating emotions such as fear, urgency, and curiosity to trick individuals into granting access. Thus, even as defenses grow stronger, the human element remains a consistent weak link. The evolution of threats in a hyperconnected era reveals an uncomfortable truth: security must adapt as quickly as the attackers evolve. Static defenses and outdated approaches are insufficient in a world where threats adapt in real time. This understanding drives the need for a proactive mindset, one that anticipates threats before they manifest and prioritizes resilience over simple defense. Without this evolution in mindset, the battle against cyber threats becomes one-sided in favor of the adversaries.

The Psychology of Attackers and Defenders

To outsmart hackers before they strike, one must first understand the psychology that drives them. Attackers are not merely faceless entities hidden behind screens; they are motivated individuals or groups with specific goals, strategies, and mindsets. Their behavior is often driven by a mix of financial gain, curiosity, power, ideology, or revenge. This diversity in motivation influences the tactics they employ. A financially motivated attacker, for example, may rely heavily on ransomware or phishing campaigns, while a politically motivated actor may aim to deface websites, leak sensitive documents, or cause reputational damage. Regardless of their specific motives, what unites attackers is their ability to exploit weaknesses creatively and persistently. The psychology of attackers revolves around asymmetry. They require only one successful attempt to infiltrate a system, while defenders must protect every possible entry point at all times. This imbalance creates a psychological advantage for attackers, as they can innovate continuously and test defenses without bearing the full cost of failure. The thrill of outsmarting a system, coupled with the anonymity of cyberspace, fuels persistence. Many attackers perceive hacking as a game of intellect where success brings a sense of dominance and accomplishment. In organized groups or state-sponsored units, these motivations are supplemented by financial rewards or nationalistic duty, further strengthening their determination. Defenders, on the other hand, operate with an entirely different psychological burden. Their role is often reactive, requiring vigilance, discipline, and patience. The responsibility of protecting valuable assets, sensitive data, and the trust of stakeholders weighs heavily on their decision-making. Unlike attackers, defenders rarely receive recognition for the attacks they prevent. Instead, failures are amplified, as even a single breach can overshadow years of quiet success. This creates an environment of constant pressure, leading to fatigue and sometimes complacency. Understanding this psychological disparity is crucial because it reveals why attackers often seem one step ahead. The mindset of defenders must shift from passive reaction to proactive anticipation. This requires cultivating an adversarial mindset, one where defenders think like attackers to anticipate moves before they happen. Ethical hacking and red teaming exercises embody this principle by simulating attacks to identify weaknesses before malicious actors can exploit them. By immersing themselves in the psychology of attackers, defenders gain valuable insights into likely strategies, making their own defenses stronger and more adaptive. The psychology of both sides is also influenced by trust and perception. Attackers thrive when they can manipulate trust, whether through phishing emails that appear legitimate or social engineering calls that impersonate authority figures. Defenders, in turn, must build environments where trust is validated continuously rather than assumed blindly. The concept of zero trust architectures reflects this shift, where no user or device is trusted by default, even if they operate within the network perimeter. This model acknowledges that attackers may already be inside and that defense requires skepticism as a psychological strategy. Ultimately, the psychology of attackers and defenders reveals a battle of creativity versus discipline. Attackers innovate, adapt, and exploit unpredictability, while defenders must anticipate, prepare, and sustain resilience. Outsmarting hackers requires not only technological defenses but also a deep psychological understanding of adversaries. To think like them, one must step into their shoes, understand their motivations, and predict their moves. The defender who internalizes the psychology of the attacker stands a greater chance of neutralizing threats before they materialize.

Building Proactive Resilience in Organizations

In an era where threats evolve rapidly and attackers exploit both technological and human weaknesses, building proactive resilience within organizations becomes the defining strategy for survival. Resilience is not merely about preventing attacks but about ensuring continuity and recovery when breaches occur. The old paradigm of building impenetrable walls around networks is obsolete; what matters today is the ability to adapt, respond, and recover faster than attackers can exploit. This resilience must be embedded into the DNA of organizations, shaping culture, policies, and practices from the ground up. Proactive resilience begins with cultivating awareness. Every member of an organization, from executives to entry-level employees, must understand the role they play in cybersecurity. Training programs that go beyond surface-level compliance are essential, creating an environment where individuals recognize phishing attempts, practice good password hygiene, and adopt secure habits. Awareness transforms employees from potential weak links into the first line of defense. However, awareness alone is insufficient without leadership commitment. Executives must view cybersecurity not as an IT problem but as a business priority. By embedding security into strategic decision-making, organizations create a culture where resilience is valued as highly as profitability. Technological investments are also central to resilience. Modern organizations must leverage advanced tools such as artificial intelligence-driven monitoring systems, threat intelligence platforms, and automated incident response solutions. These tools enable defenders to identify anomalies quickly and respond to threats in real time. Yet technology must be paired with robust processes. Incident response plans, tested regularly through simulations, prepare teams to act decisively under pressure. Without rehearsed plans, panic often replaces coordination during real incidents, leading to avoidable damage. Resilience further requires diversification and redundancy. Just as natural ecosystems survive because of their adaptability, organizations must ensure that critical functions are not reliant on single points of failure. Backup systems, cloud redundancies, and segmented networks prevent a single breach from cascading into widespread collapse. The ability to isolate compromised systems while maintaining core functions defines the difference between organizations that survive attacks and those that succumb. Proactivity is the final ingredient. Instead of waiting for attacks, organizations must hunt for threats actively. Threat hunting teams, penetration testing exercises, and partnerships with external security experts ensure continuous evaluation of defenses. By simulating the perspective of attackers, organizations identify vulnerabilities before they are exploited. Proactivity also extends to intelligence sharing, where industries collaborate to share insights about emerging threats. Cyber resilience thrives when organizations recognize that collective defense is stronger than isolated efforts. Ultimately, building proactive resilience means accepting that breaches are inevitable, but devastation is not. The mindset shifts from fearing attacks to preparing for them. An organization with resilience weathers attacks with minimal disruption, retains the trust of its stakeholders, and emerges stronger from adversity. Outsmarting hackers before they strike is not always about blocking every attempt but about ensuring that when the inevitable occurs, the damage is contained, recovery is swift, and continuity is preserved. In this sense, resilience is not a defensive posture but a competitive advantage in the hyperconnected era.

CHAPTER 6

The Anatomy of Zero Day Vulnerabilities

Zero day vulnerabilities represent one of the most feared categories of cyber threats because they are flaws that exist within systems, applications, or devices that are unknown to the vendor and therefore unpatched. The name zero day comes from the fact that once the vulnerability is discovered and weaponized, defenders have zero days to prepare against it. Unlike threats that exploit known weaknesses with available patches, zero day attacks thrive on surprise, stealth, and the inability of defenders to anticipate them. To truly outsmart hackers before they strike, one must understand the anatomy of zero day vulnerabilities in all their complexity, from their discovery to their exploitation, and eventually to their patching and mitigation. At the core of zero day vulnerabilities is the gap between innovation and security. Software developers are under constant pressure to release new features, enhance functionality, and maintain compatibility across devices and platforms. In this relentless cycle of innovation, errors inevitably occur. A simple coding oversight, an overlooked logical flaw, or an untested configuration can create a hidden entry point into the system. These flaws may remain unnoticed for months or even years until an attacker stumble upon them. Hackers, especially those aligned with organized groups or state actors, actively seek these blind spots using advanced tools and methodologies. When they find one, the race begins between exploitation and disclosure.

The discovery of a zero day vulnerability can occur in several ways. Independent researchers often uncover them while analyzing software for weaknesses, sometimes reporting them responsibly through bug bounty programs or coordinated disclosure frameworks. Unfortunately, not all discoveries are reported ethically. Some researchers choose to sell their findings on underground markets where vulnerabilities are auctioned to the highest bidder. Nation states with offensive cyber programs may hoard vulnerabilities for strategic purposes, using them in espionage or sabotage campaigns. Cybercriminals see them as lucrative opportunities to bypass defenses and compromise systems at scale. Once weaponized, a zero day vulnerability becomes a powerful tool capable of bypassing antivirus programs, intrusion detection systems, and traditional firewalls. The exploitation process is equally complex. An attacker crafts an exploit designed to take advantage of the specific weakness, often embedding it within a piece of malware or using it as part of a broader campaign. Because the vulnerability is unknown to the vendor, defenders have little to no ability to detect or block the exploit. The most dangerous zero day attacks are those that combine stealth with persistence, infiltrating a system silently and remaining undetected for long periods while exfiltrating data or establishing backdoors. In many cases, organizations only become aware of a zero day exploitation after noticing unusual activity or after security researchers publish findings. The impact of zero day vulnerabilities can be catastrophic. They have been used to target critical infrastructure, disrupt global supply chains, and compromise government agencies. One of the most famous examples is the Stuxnet worm, which leveraged multiple zero day vulnerabilities to sabotage Iranian nuclear facilities, demonstrating the geopolitical power of such attacks. Similarly, zero day exploits have been used to target financial institutions, healthcare providers, and technology companies, highlighting their broad appeal to attackers across different industries. From the defender's perspective, mitigating zero day vulnerabilities requires a mindset shift. Since they cannot be patched in advance, organizations must adopt layered defenses and focus on detection, containment, and resilience. Behavior-based monitoring systems, which identify unusual patterns rather than known signatures, are essential in identifying potential zero day activity. Network segmentation prevents attackers from moving laterally once they gain initial access. Regular updates, while not a defense against zero days themselves, minimize exposure to known vulnerabilities, reducing the attack surface. Finally, collaboration between security researchers, vendors, and organizations is critical in ensuring that once zero day vulnerabilities are discovered, patches are developed and distributed quickly. Understanding the anatomy of zero day vulnerabilities reveals an uncomfortable truth: perfection in software development is unattainable, and as long as code is written by humans, flaws will exist. Outsmarting hackers in this domain requires resilience, preparedness, and proactive defense strategies that anticipate the inevitability of the unknown.

The Economics of Exploits and the Dark Market

The persistence and danger of zero day vulnerabilities cannot be separated from the economic forces that sustain their exploitation. Behind every exploit lies a thriving market where vulnerabilities are bought, sold, and traded like commodities. This underground economy transforms technical flaws into valuable assets, incentivizing hackers and researchers to discover and weaponize vulnerabilities rather than disclose them for the public good. To understand why zero day threats, remain so prevalent, one must examine the economics that fuel their existence and the dark ecosystem that thrives on them. At the heart of this economy is scarcity. A zero day vulnerability is by definition unknown, making it highly valuable because it provides exclusive access to a target system. The rarity of such flaws ensures that demand remains high, particularly among nation states and organized criminal groups. Prices for zero day exploits vary depending on the target system's importance and prevalence. For instance, a vulnerability in a widely used operating system like Windows or Android commands a far higher price than one in a niche application. Similarly, flaws that enable remote code execution without user interaction are valued more than those requiring user involvement, because they allow attackers to compromise systems with minimal effort. The underground markets where these vulnerabilities are traded operate in secrecy. Access often requires vetting and reputation, with forums existing on the dark web protected by encryption and anonymity networks. Vendors advertise their discoveries with technical descriptions and proof-of-concept demonstrations, attracting buyers who may range from cybercriminal gangs to government agencies. In some cases, brokers act as intermediaries, connecting researchers with buyers and ensuring trust within a market that thrives on discretion. These markets have grown increasingly professional, with structured pricing, customer support, and even guarantees of exclusivity. The financial incentives are enormous. Bug bounty programs run by legitimate companies may pay tens of thousands of dollars for responsibly disclosed vulnerabilities, but underground markets often offer hundreds of thousands or even millions for the most valuable exploits. This disparity tempts many researchers to sell their findings illicitly rather than through ethical channels. The economics are simple: the black market pays more, and buyers often demand absolute secrecy, increasing the strategic value of the exploit.

Nation states play a unique role in this economy. Governments invest heavily in acquiring zero day vulnerabilities to strengthen their cyber arsenals, sometimes stockpiling them for years. This stockpiling raises ethical concerns because vulnerabilities remain unpatched, leaving millions of users exposed while governments preserve them for potential offensive use. The revelation of such practices has fueled debates about the responsibility of governments to disclose vulnerabilities to vendors versus their interest in retaining strategic advantages.

The economics of zero day exploits also highlight the challenges of deterrence. As long as vulnerabilities can be monetized, individuals and groups will continue to seek them out. Efforts to reduce this market include strengthening bug bounty programs, increasing collaboration between researchers and vendors, and developing policies that discourage governments from hoarding vulnerabilities. However, the profitability of the underground economy makes complete eradication unlikely. For defenders, understanding the economic drivers behind zero day exploits underscores the importance of continuous vigilance. The value placed on vulnerabilities means attackers will always seek them, and defenders must assume their existence even when no exploit is publicly known. Adopting a zero-trust mindset, investing in proactive threat intelligence, and participating in collaborative security networks are vital steps in countering the economic engine that fuels exploitation. Ultimately, the fight against zero-day exploits is not only technological but also economic, requiring systemic changes to shift incentives away from secrecy and toward disclosure.

Strategies for Outsmarting Zero Day Attacks

The inevitability of zero day vulnerabilities forces organizations to adopt strategies that go beyond traditional security measures. Since it is impossible to prevent flaws from existing, the focus shifts toward outsmarting attackers by anticipating their moves, minimizing potential damage, and responding with speed and precision. Outsmarting zero day attacks requires a holistic approach that integrates technology, process, culture, and collaboration into a unified defense strategy. One of the most effective strategies lies in adopting behavior-based detection systems. Unlike signature-based tools that identify known threats, behavior-based systems analyze patterns of activity to detect anomalies. For example, if a user suddenly downloads large amounts of data outside normal working hours, the system flags this as suspicious, even if no known malware signature is detected. Machine learning enhances this capability by continuously refining models based on evolving behaviors, enabling organizations to spot subtle indicators of zero day exploitation. Another critical strategy is network segmentation. By dividing networks into isolated zones, organizations reduce the ability of attackers to move laterally once inside. Even if a zero day vulnerability is exploited to breach one segment, the damage is contained, preventing access to critical systems. Similarly, implementing the principle of least privilege ensures that users and devices only have the minimum access necessary to perform their functions, limiting the potential impact of compromised accounts. Proactive threat hunting is also essential. Instead of waiting for alerts, dedicated teams search actively for signs of compromise, analyzing logs, traffic, and user behavior to uncover hidden threats. This adversarial approach mirrors the mindset of attackers, allowing organizations to identify weaknesses before they are exploited. Regular penetration testing and red teaming exercises complement this effort, exposing vulnerabilities in a controlled environment.

Resilience plays a central role in outsmarting zero day attacks. This means preparing for breaches through well-defined incident response plans, regular backups, and disaster recovery strategies. Organizations must rehearse their response to ensure that when an attack occurs, they can act decisively rather than reactively. Swift containment, communication, and recovery minimize both operational disruption and reputational damage. Collaboration across industries is another indispensable strategy. Since zero day vulnerabilities can impact multiple organizations simultaneously, sharing intelligence about emerging threats strengthens collective defense. Industry groups, information-sharing platforms, and partnerships between private and public sectors enable faster identification and mitigation of exploits. Ultimately, the mindset required to outsmart zero day attacks is one of proactive adaptation. Organizations must accept that zero day vulnerabilities will always exist, but they must refuse to be caught unprepared. By blending advanced detection technologies, segmented architectures, proactive hunting, resilience planning, and collaborative intelligence, defenders can neutralize the advantage attackers gain from the unknown. Outsmarting hackers before they strike does not mean eliminating vulnerabilities but ensuring that when they are exploited, defenders respond with such speed and foresight that attackers fail to achieve their objectives.

CHAPTER 7

Understanding the Hacker Mindset

The battle for cybersecurity is never just about codes or systems it is equally about the psychology of the actors on both sides of the divide because hackers operate with a unique blend of curiosity persistence and audacity they are not always driven by money or recognition sometimes it is the thrill of discovery the desire to test limits and the hunger to outsmart the invisible walls of security that fuels their actions understanding this mindset is critical because it reveals why traditional defenses that are built around compliance and rules often fail to anticipate attacks hackers thrive on unpredictability and when organizations adopt predictable routines or outdated models they essentially open doors that invite exploitation the hacker mindset is marked by asymmetrical thinking where small resources can be leveraged to achieve disproportionately large outcomes this asymmetry means a single attacker in a remote location can compromise multinational organizations by identifying a single overlooked vulnerability they thrive on exploiting assumptions such as the belief that low level systems are unimportant or that obscure entry points are safe but for hackers the ignored corner is often the treasure chest the hacker psyche is also marked by a disregard for boundaries what a company sees as separate systems a hacker sees as interconnected opportunities what an organization views as isolated issues hackers see as part of a larger pattern their strength lies in connecting the dots where defenders fail to make associations hackers spend endless hours exploring systems not because they must but because they want to they often enjoy the process of reverse engineering probing weaknesses and testing possibilities where others see obstacles they see puzzles this psychological drive makes them relentless because they do not stop when they encounter obstacles they adapt until they find new routes and this resilience makes them formidable opponents it is this spirit of persistence that defenders must study not only to anticipate the nature of attacks but to emulate the same level of focus and creativity on the defensive side without understanding how attackers think defenders risk being perpetually one step behind

Building the Defensive Mindset

If the hacker mindset thrives on asymmetry and relentless curiosity then the defensive mindset must be built upon anticipation resilience and disciplined innovation defenders must learn not to think like bureaucrats but like strategists who see threats before they materialize yet unlike hackers who are often free from constraints defenders must operate within organizational limits regulatory frameworks and finite resources this creates a paradox because defenders are asked to secure everything while attackers only need to succeed once therefore the defensive mindset requires clarity of priorities defenders must know which assets are most valuable which systems represent critical vulnerabilities and where the cost of compromise is highest without this clarity efforts are diluted and resources are wasted on the wrong battles a disciplined defender views systems not in isolation but as living ecosystems that evolve over time they recognize that each new device connection or application introduces both opportunity and vulnerability the defensive mindset is not simply about monitoring but about pattern recognition defenders must develop the ability to connect seemingly unrelated anomalies to form a larger picture of potential compromise much like chess players they must see the board several moves ahead while simultaneously guarding against distractions the psychological strength of a defender lies in patience because security is a long game where prevention may not yield visible results unlike the visible success of a hacker who compromises a system defenders succeed in silence when nothing happens yet this silence must not lead to complacency defenders must cultivate internal motivation driven by the knowledge that unseen effort prevents unseen disasters this defensive psychology also requires resilience because no system can be perfect breaches are inevitable and when they happen defenders must avoid despair or blame instead they must act with speed coordination and clarity to contain the threat and restore trust a defensive mindset does not end with technology it also extends to culture defenders must work to instill awareness across every level of the organization so that security becomes part of collective behavior rather than the responsibility of a few specialists without this cultural integration even the best technical defenses will eventually crumble because human error is the gateway through which most attacks succeed If the hacker mindset thrives on asymmetry and relentless curiosity then the defensive mindset must be built upon anticipation resilience and disciplined innovation defenders must learn not to think like bureaucrats but like strategists who see threats before they materialize yet unlike hackers who are often free from constraints defenders must operate within organizational limits regulatory frameworks and finite resources this creates a paradox because defenders are asked to secure everything while attackers only need to succeed once therefore the defensive mindset requires clarity of priorities defenders must know which assets are most valuable which systems represent critical vulnerabilities and where the cost of compromise is highest without this clarity efforts are diluted and resources are wasted on the wrong battles a disciplined defender views systems not in isolation but as living ecosystems that evolve over time they recognize that each new device connection or application introduces both opportunity and vulnerability the defensive mindset is not simply about monitoring but about pattern recognition defenders must develop the ability to connect seemingly unrelated anomalies to form a larger picture of potential compromise much like chess players they must see the board several moves ahead while simultaneously guarding against distractions the psychological strength of a defender lies in patience because security is a long game where prevention may not yield visible results unlike the visible success of a hacker who compromises a system defenders succeed in silence when nothing happens yet this silence must not lead to complacency defenders must cultivate internal motivation driven by the knowledge that unseen effort prevents unseen disasters this defensive psychology also requires resilience because no system can be perfect breaches are inevitable and when they happen defenders must avoid despair or blame instead they must act with speed coordination and clarity to contain the threat and restore trust a defensive mindset does not end with technology it also extends to culture defenders must work to instill awareness across every level of the organization so that security becomes part of collective behavior rather than the responsibility of a few specialists without this cultural integration even the best technical defenses will eventually crumble because human error is the gateway through which most attacks succeed the strength of a defensive mindset also lies in adaptability because attackers evolve daily and any defense that stands still becomes obsolete defenders must cultivate an attitude of constant learning updating skills policies and technologies to keep pace with evolving threats they must encourage curiosity within their teams so that defenders are not simply following checklists but actively probing their own systems for weaknesses a culture of red teaming where defenders simulate attacks against themselves helps build this mindset of constant anticipation by thinking like attackers defenders sharpen their ability to anticipate moves before they happen the defensive mindset must also embrace collaboration because no single individual or organization can secure the digital world alone information sharing across industries sectors and nations becomes essential when one company is attacked and learns from the incident that knowledge should strengthen others the more defenders learn collectively the less room attackers have to exploit isolation defenders must also fight overconfidence because one of the greatest psychological vulnerabilities of defenders is the belief that their systems are impenetrable history shows that no matter how advanced defenses become attackers eventually find ways in humility must therefore be at the heart of the defensive mindset because humility fuels vigilance while arrogance fuels neglect another important component of building the defensive mindset is balance defenders cannot focus exclusively on external threats while ignoring internal risks insiders whether malicious or negligent remain one of the greatest dangers to organizations a defensive mindset treats trust carefully not as blind confidence but as measured verification access control segmentation and auditing ensure that trust does not become a liability defenders must also recognize that speed is critical in modern security the days when breaches unfolded slowly have been replaced by lightning fast attacks where minutes can determine whether data is stolen or systems are crippled therefore defenders must design response strategies that emphasize speed of detection speed of communication and speed of containment but speed must never come at the cost of clarity because rushing blindly can amplify mistakes thus the defensive mindset values both urgency and accuracy another often overlooked aspect of the defensive mindset is the importance of psychology within defensive teams defenders face a unique pressure because their work is defined by preventing invisible threats and when they succeed their success often goes unrecognized unlike hackers who enjoy the thrill of visible victory defenders operate in the shadows this lack of recognition can lead to burnout and frustration therefore leadership must reinforce the value of defenders ensuring their efforts are acknowledged and celebrated otherwise morale declines and with it the sharpness of defense defenders must also understand that their ultimate mission is not to create perfect security which is impossible but to build resilience that allows organizations to absorb attacks recover quickly and continue functioning resilience requires backups redundancy continuity planning and clear communication because in the face of crisis organizations that can remain calm and restore order quickly retain trust while those that crumble under pressure lose credibility alongside data resilience is therefore both technical and psychological a defensive mindset sees every incident as an opportunity to strengthen rather than as a failure to prevent the ability to adapt and learn from attacks ensures that each breach makes the system stronger not weaker ultimately the defensive mindset is not about reacting to threats but about shaping the environment in ways that minimize opportunities for attackers when defenders embrace foresight discipline resilience and humility they tilt the balance of power in their favor even against adversaries who thrive on asymmetry the future belongs to defenders who understand that security is not a state but a practice not an outcome but a journey and not a burden but the very foundation of trust in the digital world.

Psychological Warfare in the Digital Arena

The intersection of the hacker mindset and the defensive mindset creates a battleground defined not just by tools but by psychology because each side seeks to outthink the other hackers exploit fear uncertainty and ignorance they often use psychological manipulation to achieve technical goals through social engineering phishing and disinformation campaigns they prey on human emotions such as trust urgency and curiosity to bypass technological defenses attackers know that the easiest way into a system is often through the mind of an employee rather than the code of a machine they weaponize narratives convincing targets to click on malicious links to surrender credentials or to reveal sensitive information believing they are helping a legitimate cause this is psychological warfare in its purest form because it turns human behavior into a weapon defenders must therefore treat psychology not as a secondary concern but as a frontline battleground defense strategies must incorporate training awareness and simulations that expose individuals to the tricks and tactics of manipulation only when employees experience the deceptive realism of phishing campaigns or staged breaches do they develop the skepticism and caution that protects organizations at scale defenders must also fight psychological fatigue within their own ranks because cybersecurity professionals are constantly bombarded by alerts threats and endless responsibilities burnout becomes a real danger and hackers count on fatigue to weaken defenses thus leaders must invest not only in systems but in the mental health and resilience of their defenders providing rest training and mental clarity to ensure their teams remain sharp the future of cybersecurity will increasingly be shaped by this psychological warfare because as artificial intelligence automates many technical aspects the human mind will remain the ultimate frontier it is in the realm of perception trust and decision making where victories and defeats will be decided understanding this reality ensures that defenders are not blindsided by attacks that bypass firewalls not with code but with carefully crafted lies in the digital age the greatest battlefield is the mind and those who master its dynamics will hold the true power. The intersection of the hacker mindset and the defensive mindset creates a battleground defined not just by tools but by psychology because each side seeks to outthink the other hackers exploit fear uncertainty and ignorance they often use psychological manipulation to achieve technical goals through social engineering phishing and disinformation campaigns they prey on human emotions such as trust urgency and curiosity to bypass technological defenses attackers know that the easiest way into a system is often through the mind of an employee rather than the code of a machine they weaponize narratives convincing targets to click on malicious links to surrender credentials or to reveal sensitive information believing they are helping a legitimate cause this is psychological warfare in its purest form because it turns human behavior into a weapon defenders must therefore treat psychology not as a secondary concern but as a frontline battleground defense strategies must incorporate training awareness and simulations that expose individuals to the tricks and tactics of manipulation only when employees experience the deceptive realism of phishing campaigns or staged breaches do they develop the skepticism and caution that protects organizations at scale defenders must also fight psychological fatigue within their own ranks because cybersecurity professionals are constantly bombarded by alerts threats and endless responsibilities burnout becomes a real danger and hackers count on fatigue to weaken defenses thus leaders must invest not only in systems but in the mental health and resilience of their defenders providing rest training and mental clarity to ensure their teams remain sharp the future of cybersecurity will increasingly be shaped by this psychological warfare because as artificial intelligence automates many technical aspects the human mind will remain the ultimate frontier it is in the realm of perception trust and decision making where victories and defeats will be decided understanding this reality ensures that defenders are not blindsided by attacks that bypass firewalls not with code but with carefully crafted lies in the digital age the greatest battlefield is the mind and those who master its dynamics will hold the true power the sophistication of modern psychological attacks cannot be underestimated because cyber adversaries are no longer limited to simple email scams they employ layered tactics that weave together misinformation social trends and cultural narratives attackers study their targets with precision they analyze behavior patterns online habits and even social relationships to craft personalized attacks known as spear phishing these attacks are far more dangerous than broad attempts because they speak directly to the vulnerabilities of individuals and they rely on familiarity trust and relevance to lower defenses for example an employee might ignore a generic phishing attempt but they may respond immediately to an email that references a recent project meeting a known colleague or even a personal interest gleaned from social media this targeted form of psychological manipulation shows how attackers do not need to break systems when they can break people with subtle influence defenders must therefore integrate behavioral analytics into their security strategies by monitoring for anomalies not just in systems but in human actions an employee who suddenly begins transferring unusual amounts of data or engaging with strange links should raise alerts that are not ignored because they signal a compromise of behavior as much as of technology at the same time defenders must grapple with the rise of disinformation as a weapon entire campaigns are now engineered not only to steal data but to destabilize societies attackers spread rumors online manipulate trending topics and manufacture fake accounts to influence public opinion this kind of psychological warfare targets collective behavior at scale rather than individual actions and its danger lies in its ability to erode trust in institutions when people begin doubting the authenticity of what they see or hear they become vulnerable to manipulation that weakens democratic structures businesses and entire economies in this sense cyber warfare is no longer confined to firewalls it has expanded into the domain of perception defenders must respond by developing resilience strategies that go beyond technology building media literacy programs training individuals to question sources and equipping communities with the tools to resist manipulation without such awareness societies risk losing not just data but their ability to make informed decisions another dimension of psychological warfare is the exploitation of urgency hackers craft messages that demand immediate action because they know urgency shuts down critical thinking when someone is told their account will be locked unless they act within minutes or that a payment must be confirmed urgently they are more likely to make mistakes defenders must therefore train people to resist urgency by building habits of verification rather than reaction because the strongest shield is not speed but clarity of mind furthermore psychological warfare thrives on authority attackers often impersonate figures of power such as executives managers or government officials in order to manipulate compliance employees who would normally resist suspicious instructions often obey when the message appears to come from authority this tendency highlights the need for defenders to design protocols where authority is verified rather than assumed because unchecked trust in hierarchy is an open door for exploitation in addition hackers exploit curiosity the innate human desire to know more to click links to open attachments or to uncover surprises this curiosity is one of the oldest vulnerabilities and yet one of the hardest to control it cannot be eliminated but it can be redirected defenders can train individuals to channel curiosity into safer actions such as testing suspicious files in secure environments rather than opening them directly the goal is not to kill curiosity but to discipline it so that it does not become a weapon in the wrong hands the psychological dimension of cyber warfare is not limited to civilians it extends to the defenders themselves hackers often attempt to demoralize or distract security teams by launching waves of low level attacks that flood systems with noise the intention is not always to break through but to exhaust defenders to occupy their attention and create blind spots during which a more significant attack is launched this strategy plays on the psychology of fatigue defenders must develop counter strategies such as automated filtering prioritization and stress management to avoid falling into these traps because a distracted or exhausted defender is as vulnerable as an untrained employee looking ahead the next frontier of psychological warfare will likely merge artificial intelligence with manipulation at scale attackers will deploy algorithms that craft personalized messages for millions of individuals simultaneously adapting to responses in real time and refining persuasion techniques with machine precision this could transform phishing from a crude tool into a hyper personalized psychological campaign capable of overwhelming defenses defenders will need to match this sophistication with their own use of artificial intelligence to detect subtle behavioral anomalies across networks while simultaneously investing in the human side of resilience because no matter how advanced machines become the human mind will remain the ultimate target in this ongoing conflict the lesson is clear the most advanced firewalls and encryption methods cannot protect an organization if its people are unprepared because the true weapon of the hacker is not only in their code but in their ability to control perception to distort trust and to exploit the fragile nature of human psychology the digital battlefield has therefore evolved from a war of machines into a war of minds and in this theater the side that invests in education awareness and psychological resilience will always hold the upper ground.

CHAPTER 8

The Invisible Economy of Cybercrime

Cybercrime is not just a collection of isolated attacks it is a thriving economy that mirrors legitimate markets in both structure and function operating silently in the shadows this invisible economy drives much of the malicious activity that organizations and individuals face daily hackers are not merely hobbyists or rogue agents they are participants in an interconnected marketplace where data exploits and services are traded like commodities understanding this economy requires an exploration of its layers because it is organized with surprising sophistication much like any global enterprise at the top tier there are developers who create tools malware and exploit kits they operate as producers providing the raw materials of cybercrime beneath them are distributors who package these tools for resale adapting them for specific audiences and ensuring they are accessible to both skilled and unskilled actors further down the chain lie the operators who execute attacks using purchased tools ranging from ransomware campaigns to phishing operations at the bottom are the consumers individuals or groups who buy stolen data credentials or illicit services for profit or personal use this layered structure demonstrates that cybercrime is not a random collection of chaotic acts but a systemized economy driven by demand and supply data is the currency of this economy and it is valued according to its utility and rarity personal credentials credit card details medical records and intellectual property are all priced differently depending on how quickly and effectively they can be monetized for instance credit card data is abundant and loses value quickly once reported stolen while medical records retain long term value because they contain stable personal information that can be exploited for identity theft or fraud for years intellectual property such as trade secrets or source code can command premium prices because they provide competitive advantage to buyers in black markets the methods of payment within this economy are equally important cryptocurrencies particularly those offering anonymity are the lifeblood of cybercrime transactions bitcoin initially fueled this shift by enabling relatively anonymous transfers but newer currencies with stronger privacy protections have increasingly taken the lead this reliance on cryptocurrencies reveals the adaptability of cybercriminals who leverage innovations from the legitimate financial sector to fuel their underground operations yet the economy of cybercrime is not limited to trade in data and tools it also encompasses services such as ransomware as a service where sophisticated operators lease out their attack infrastructures to less skilled individuals for a percentage of the profits this franchise like model lowers the barrier to entry enabling more actors to participate and expanding the scale of global cybercrime it also mirrors legitimate business models with pricing tiers customer support and updates showing that in the underground economy professionalism thrives alongside illegality the invisible economy of cybercrime is further reinforced by reputation systems attackers establish credibility through consistent delivery and reliability just like sellers on legitimate platforms if a vendor consistently provides working exploits or valid stolen data they build trust within the community and can charge premium rates this reliance on reputation highlights the paradox of trust within an untrustworthy environment where actors must rely on each other's reliability to sustain business transactions this paradoxical trust system makes the underground economy surprisingly resilient despite its illegality understanding the scale and sophistication of this invisible economy reveals why cybercrime continues to grow unchecked it is not merely a threat from isolated hackers but a vast interconnected system that mirrors the legitimate economy and thrives on the weaknesses of modern technology and human behavior

Black Markets and the Trade of Digital Goods

The black markets where cybercriminals trade are the digital equivalent of bustling marketplaces though hidden from the surface web they are accessible to those who know where to look operating on the dark web through anonymizing technologies these markets facilitate the exchange of goods and services ranging from stolen data to malware to counterfeit documents what makes these markets formidable is their resilience because even when law enforcement shuts down one platform another quickly emerges often more sophisticated and harder to track the trade of digital goods in these markets is governed by supply demand and reputation stolen credit cards sell in bulk at low prices while rare credentials such as administrative access to corporate systems command higher rates these credentials are particularly valuable because they provide direct entry into secure environments enabling attackers to launch devastating intrusions with minimal effort databases containing thousands of personal records are another commodity and they are sold by volume the larger the dataset the higher the price although quality matters because invalid or outdated information reduces value some markets specialize in niche goods such as intellectual property proprietary software or zero day exploits these highly prized commodities are scarce and their value skyrockets depending on their potential impact a zero day exploit capable of compromising widely used systems can sell for millions placing it on par with high stakes commodities in the legitimate world the structure of these black markets often mirrors legitimate e commerce platforms they include product descriptions vendor ratings customer reviews and dispute resolution mechanisms creating a veneer of professionalism that fosters trust in an environment otherwise rife with deception buyers can search browse and select products with the same ease as on mainstream online retailers except here the products are illicit data and digital tools of destruction payments are conducted using cryptocurrencies ensuring a layer of anonymity although sophisticated buyers and sellers employ additional measures such as mixers tumblers and privacy coins to further obscure financial trails beyond goods and services these markets offer communities where knowledge is exchanged forums enable hackers to share techniques discuss vulnerabilities and mentor newcomers this flow of knowledge accelerates the evolution of cybercrime making it more difficult for defenders to keep pace newcomers can quickly acquire the tools and knowledge necessary to launch attacks without years of experience or deep technical expertise transforming cybercrime from an elite pursuit into a mainstream underground industry law enforcement agencies have attempted to infiltrate and dismantle these markets with varying success operations that take down major platforms often create temporary disruption but rarely long term collapse because the underlying demand persists like cutting the head off a hydra shutting down one platform often results in the rise of multiple successors more agile and elusive than their predecessors this adaptability ensures the resilience of black markets and makes them a persistent challenge for global security the trade of digital goods in these markets has significant real world consequences every stolen identity leads to financial loss every leaked record erodes trust every compromised system weakens the integrity of businesses and governments the persistence of these markets demonstrates that cybercrime is not a sporadic occurrence but an entrenched industry feeding on the vulnerabilities of the digital era

The Cost of Cybercrime to Society

The economic cost of cybercrime extends far beyond the transactions of black markets it ripples through businesses governments and individuals creating a financial and social burden that undermines trust innovation and stability businesses face direct costs from attacks including ransom payments data recovery expenses regulatory fines and legal liabilities yet the indirect costs are often even greater because they involve lost customer trust damaged reputations and disrupted operations a single breach can cause years of reputational harm undermining confidence in an organization's ability to safeguard its stakeholders for small and medium enterprises the cost of an attack can be catastrophic often leading to closure because they lack the resources to recover governments bear significant burdens as well because cybercrime undermines national security drains public funds and destabilizes economies state resources must be diverted toward investigations prevention and international collaboration all of which require significant investment yet these costs are often reactive expenditures because governments are compelled to spend after breaches have occurred rather than investing proactively in systems of resilience individuals to pay the price for cybercrime identity theft ruins lives by entangling victims in long battles to reclaim their financial credibility the theft of medical records compromises privacy at the most personal level and the loss of savings through fraudulent schemes creates emotional trauma that far exceeds monetary damage the societal cost is also psychological because widespread reports of breaches create a climate of fear and uncertainty when people lose trust in digital systems they hesitate to adopt new technologies slowing innovation and limiting the potential of digital transformation entire industries suffer as hesitation replaces confidence and reluctance replaces enthusiasm the broader economy is therefore weakened not just by direct theft but by the erosion of trust which is the lifeblood of modern commerce in addition to economic and psychological costs cybercrime fosters inequality because victims are often those least equipped to recover marginalized individuals small businesses and under resourced institutions face the greatest harm while wealthy entities can absorb losses and move forward this unequal distribution of impact deepens social divides creating a digital environment where vulnerability is disproportionately borne by those with the fewest defenses the cost to society also includes the diversion of innovation resources when companies are forced to spend heavily on security they have fewer resources to invest in research development and creative projects security becomes a tax on innovation necessary yet burdensome the paradox is that the same digital technologies that empower progress also require constant vigilance draining energy that could otherwise be used for advancement at the macroeconomic level cybercrime undermines global trust in financial systems trade and communication the cross border nature of attacks makes attribution and accountability difficult leading to political tensions and mistrust among nations the result is a digital environment where suspicion replaces cooperation and where the potential for global collaboration is weakened by the constant threat of unseen adversaries ultimately the cost of cybercrime to society cannot be measured only in currency it must also be measured in lost opportunities in broken trust and in the weakening of the social fabric that binds digital interactions together the real toll is hidden in the businesses that never recover the innovations that never launch and the people who lose faith in the promise of the digital future. The true cost of cybercrime cannot be measured only in financial terms it is a multi-layered burden that infiltrates economies destabilizes institutions weakens trust and disrupts the very fabric of society while estimates of global cybercrime costs often reach trillions of dollars annually those figures capture only a fraction of the reality because behind every statistic lies a ripple effect that extends far beyond the immediate victim when a corporation suffers a breach the first visible consequence is monetary loss from theft fraud ransom or business disruption yet beneath this surface lies a deeper erosion of confidence customers begin to doubt whether their personal information is safe investors question the resilience of the organization and markets punish perceived weakness these reactions extend far beyond one company they create an atmosphere of uncertainty where consumers hesitate to engage in digital services and where innovation slows because of fear when people are afraid to transact online the entire digital economy suffers a hidden tax that drags down growth and opportunity governments too bear enormous costs from cybercrime public services healthcare energy transportation and defense all operate on digital infrastructure when these systems are attacked it is not only money at stake but public safety and national security hospitals paralyzed by ransomware cannot deliver timely care power grids disrupted by malware can plunge entire regions into chaos election systems targeted by disinformation or intrusion can weaken democracy itself these systemic risks show that cybercrime is not a niche problem but a societal one where the consequences touch every citizen whether directly or indirectly the cost of cybercrime also manifests in the psychological domain victims of identity theft suffer long term stress trying to restore credit and reputations small businesses that collapse after a breach leave employees without jobs and communities without services societies as a whole absorb these burdens through higher prices increased insurance premiums and reduced confidence in institutions the hidden tax of cybercrime is therefore borne by everyone even those who were not direct targets education systems are also impacted schools universities and research institutions are increasingly targeted because they hold sensitive data and cutting edge knowledge when their networks are compromised the cost is not only the disruption of classes but the theft of intellectual capital that took years of investment to build this loss of innovation undermines future progress and gives adversaries an advantage in global competition the societal cost is thus measured not only in immediate disruption but in long term erosion of competitiveness at the national and global scale cybercrime also widens inequality because the wealthiest organizations can afford advanced defenses while smaller businesses individuals and public institutions remain vulnerable this creates a digital divide where opportunity is concentrated in those who can protect themselves while the rest suffer repeated losses the poor are disproportionately targeted in scams because they are more likely to fall for financial traps and less able to recover from losses thus cybercrime deepens social fractures by exploiting the vulnerable law enforcement and judicial systems bear another layer of cost as they struggle to keep pace with the global scale of cybercrime investigations are complex cross border and resource intensive the lack of jurisdictional alignment means many criminals operate with impunity leaving societies to shoulder the burden without closure this fuels frustration erodes faith in justice and creates the perception that cyberspace is lawless an environment where criminals thrive without fear the cost to society is therefore moral as well as material it diminishes collective faith in the rule of law yet perhaps the greatest societal cost of cybercrime is the erosion of trust is the invisible currency that enables digital interactions it allows people to shop bank communicate and innovate online when trust is broken it cannot be easily restored without trust digital transformation slows collaboration weakens and the very promise of the digital age is undermined societies that cannot trust their digital infrastructure are condemned to stagnation because fear replaces possibility this erosion of trust extends to governments corporations and even social relationships when disinformation spreads unchecked citizens no longer trust news or institutions and polarization deepens weakening social cohesion and democratic stability in this sense the cost of cybercrime is not simply about lost dollars but about the weakening of societal bonds themselves in sum cybercrime extracts a tax that society pays in multiple dimensions economic disruption institutional instability psychological harm weakened competitiveness inequality stressed law enforcement and above all eroded trust these costs accumulate quietly but relentlessly until they reshape how individuals organizations and nations operate in the digital world the burden is collective because the effects ripple through every layer of society and the longer it persists the more deeply it embeds itself into our future

CHAPTER 9

The Anatomy of Cyber Deception

Cyber deception is one of the most powerful yet underestimated tools in the arsenal of both attackers and defenders at its core deception manipulates perception it convinces the target to believe what is false and ignore what is true it is psychological warfare executed through digital means attackers use deception to mask their footprints to lure defenders into wasting resources and to create false confidence while defenders use deception to mislead attackers into traps to slow their progress and to study their techniques understanding the anatomy of deception begins with recognizing that cyberspace is an environment where perception can be easily manipulated unlike the physical world where tangible evidence is harder to counterfeit digital signals can be crafted fabricated or disguised with alarming precision attackers exploit this by disguising malicious payloads as harmless files by impersonating trusted identities or by simulating normal traffic to blend into background noise phishing emails are perhaps the most common form of cyber deception they exploit trust by mimicking familiar institutions or individuals and succeed not because of technical superiority but because of psychological manipulation they appeal to fear urgency or curiosity tricking the recipient into clicking a link or divulging information yet deception extends far beyond phishing advanced adversaries use fake domains decoy servers and even fabricated social media identities to build elaborate illusions in which defenders cannot easily distinguish reality from fabrication on the other hand defenders who adopt deception technology deploy honeypots honey tokens and decoy networks these are fake assets designed to attract attackers and reveal their presence the purpose is not merely to catch the intruder but to waste their time to gather intelligence on their behavior and to create a battlefield where defenders control the terrain deception shifts the balance by forcing attackers into uncertainty when they cannot tell whether a target is real or fake they hesitate and when they hesitate defenders gain the upper hand the effectiveness of deception lies in its subtlety for if it is too obvious it fails yet if it is too seamless it can completely redefine the battlefield deception is not just technical it is also strategic organizations can practice strategic deception by publishing misleading information about their security posture or by rotating infrastructure to make reconnaissance more difficult in essence the anatomy of cyber deception is about controlling perception and perception shapes decision making in a battlefield defined by information those who control perception control the fight

Psychological Manipulation in Cyber Conflict

Beyond technical deception lies the deeper layer of psychological manipulation where the human mind becomes the true target attackers understand that humans are the weakest link in any security chain and therefore design strategies not only to breach systems but to exploit emotions cognitive biases and psychological blind spots fear remains the most exploited emotion in cyber conflict a message warning that an account will be closed or that legal consequences will follow pushes individuals into hasty decisions urgency works hand in hand with fear because people under time pressure are more likely to overlook red flags curiosity is another exploited trait attackers craft lures that tempt targets into clicking links or opening attachments simply because the subject line triggers interest or excitement authority bias is also a common weapon when emails appear to come from executives or government agencies recipients are more likely to obey without question these manipulations are not random they are rooted in decades of psychological research on persuasion influence and decision making attackers apply this knowledge with precision tailoring campaigns to specific cultures demographics or even individual personalities in advanced scenarios adversaries conduct profiling to understand the fears values and habits of their targets then they craft personalized deceptions that bypass even the most vigilant defenses in this sense cyber conflict is not only technical but profoundly human defenders must therefore cultivate awareness of these manipulations within organizations training individuals to recognize emotional triggers and resist the instinctive reactions that attackers rely upon awareness programs that simulate phishing or test response to fake alerts can help inoculate users against real attacks yet training alone is insufficient defenders must also design systems that reduce opportunities for manipulation by automating responses limiting privileges and enforcing verification before sensitive actions are taken psychological manipulation also extends into the realm of information warfare where adversaries spread disinformation to destabilize societies sow distrust or influence public opinion by flooding the digital space with conflicting narratives attackers seek to overwhelm individuals' ability to discern truth from falsehood this erodes trust not only in digital platforms but in institutions themselves defenders confronting this form of manipulation face a more complex challenge because it is not merely about blocking malicious code but about strengthening societal resilience against disinformation campaigns media literacy transparency and trust building become as important as firewalls and intrusion detection in the long run psychological manipulation in cyber conflict demonstrates that the battle is not only over systems but over minds the side that masters psychology gains control over the digital arena because decisions made under manipulated perceptions shape the trajectory of conflict more than raw technical force. Psychological manipulation in cyber conflict represents one of the most insidious and complex battlegrounds of the digital age because it targets not machines but the human mind unlike purely technical attacks that exploit code or infrastructure psychological manipulation exploits perception cognition and emotion it weaponizes the vulnerabilities of human psychology and uses them to gain entry influence behavior or destabilize trust the foundation of such manipulation lies in the recognition that humans are often the weakest link in cybersecurity systems can be patched firewalls can be hardened algorithms can be improved but human behavior is unpredictable inconsistent and subject to influence from fear curiosity authority or desire this makes people the ultimate target for adversaries who seek to bypass strong defenses by exploiting the very users they protect at the most basic level psychological manipulation in cyber conflict manifests through phishing and social engineering campaigns an attacker sends an email that appears legitimate a bank request a company invoice a government warning the victim reacting to urgency fear or trust in authority responds without careful analysis thereby granting the attacker access what seems like a trivial trick is in fact the entry point for some of the most devastating breaches in history yet phishing is only the surface beneath lies a layered and evolving science of persuasion and behavioral exploitation advanced manipulation campaigns are crafted with precision often informed by data harvested from social media browsing histories and public records attackers conduct detailed reconnaissance on individuals or organizations building psychological profiles that reveal personality traits fears values and habits with this knowledge they tailor their lures to maximize the likelihood of success rather than sending generic emails they send personalized messages that resonate emotionally with the recipient the illusion is so compelling that even trained professionals sometimes fall victim manipulation in cyber conflict thrives on cognitive biases the shortcuts that humans unconsciously use to process information authority bias leads individuals to obey requests from perceived superiors attackers exploit this by impersonating executives or government officials creating what are known as business email compromise scams where subordinates transfer funds or sensitive data because they believe they are following orders confirmation bias makes people more likely to accept information that aligns with their existing beliefs attackers exploit this by crafting disinformation campaigns that reinforce polarizing views thereby deepening divisions within societies urgency bias leads individuals to act quickly when time pressure is applied attackers exploit this by creating fake deadlines threats of account closure or warnings of dire consequences if immediate action is not taken scarcity bias drives people to act when they believe opportunities are limited attackers exploit this in scams offering exclusive investments or once in a lifetime deals that pressure individuals into hasty decisions each of these biases represents a crack in human decision making and cyber manipulators exploit them with relentless precision beyond individuals psychological manipulation in cyber conflict extends to entire organizations adversaries plant seeds of doubt between departments disrupt communication channels or manipulate information to create mistrust within teams for example a manipulated insider email chain suggesting betrayal by one department may erode cooperation and delay response to a real cyber-attack sowing confusion that benefits the attacker manipulation is not only about tricking individuals into specific actions it is also about shaping long term perceptions disinformation campaigns illustrate this clearly attackers flood digital spaces with false or misleading information making it difficult for citizens to distinguish truth from falsehood over time this erodes trust in media institutions and even democracy itself the goal is not necessarily to convince people of one particular falsehood but to overwhelm them with so much conflicting information that they no longer believe anything this state of confusion serves the attacker because a society that cannot trust is a society that cannot act cohesively advanced psychological manipulation also involves emotional engineering attackers understand that strong emotions impair rational judgment fear is the most powerful tool because it triggers instinctive reactions that bypass critical thinking fear of financial loss fear of legal consequences fear of missing out fear of reputational damage all of these can be provoked through carefully crafted messages curiosity is another exploited emotion attackers lure targets into opening malicious attachments by triggering the need to know what is inside a file or behind a link pride can also be manipulated by crafting scenarios where the victim feels flattered or singled out for exclusive opportunity thereby lowering their guard even compassion can be manipulated as seen in scams where attackers pose as charities during disasters appealing to the empathy of individuals who wish to help victims yet psychological manipulation in cyber conflict does not operate solely at the individual or societal level it also affects defenders themselves attackers deliberately manipulate defenders by generating false alarms to exhaust their resources by creating noise that hides real intrusions and by timing attacks to exploit stress or fatigue this is known as cognitive overload where defenders faced with too many alerts begin to ignore or misinterpret signals attackers exploit this fatigue to slip through unnoticed in this sense manipulation is not only offensive but strategic it shapes the tempo of conflict forcing defenders to operate reactively under psychological strain in military and geopolitical contexts manipulation takes on even broader forms nation state adversaries use cyber enabled psychological operations to influence public opinion destabilize governments or weaken alliances they plant false narratives online amplify divisions through bots and fake accounts and manipulate perception of events in ways that align with their strategic goals the battlefield is not hardware but hearts and minds the weapons are not missiles but memes and misinformation campaigns the victims are not just soldiers but entire populations the long term damage is profound because it undermines social cohesion and erodes trust in democratic institutions defenders confronting psychological manipulation face challenges unlike those of traditional cybersecurity because the enemy is not only attacking technology but shaping human behavior firewalls cannot block disinformation antivirus cannot neutralize cognitive bias technical defenses alone are insufficient therefore a comprehensive response requires integrating psychology education and culture with technology individuals must be trained not only to recognize suspicious links but to understand how their emotions and biases can be exploited awareness campaigns should move beyond mechanical instruction to build emotional resilience teaching people to pause when confronted with fear urgency or flattery organizations must design environments where critical actions require verification regardless of authority where urgency is tempered by safeguards and where communication is transparent to prevent manipulation through misinformation at the societal level resilience requires education systems that cultivate media literacy populations must learn to question sources cross check information and resist the instinct to share unverified claims transparency from governments and institutions is also crucial because when truth is scarce manipulation thrives building trust requires consistent openness so that when falsehoods arise they can be countered with credible evidence swiftly defenders must also innovate in psychological countermeasures just as attackers study human behavior so too must defenders invest in understanding cognition persuasion and influence the integration of behavioral science into cybersecurity strategies is no longer optional it is essential the defensive use of psychological manipulation may even involve reverse tactics where attackers are made to question their own environment through deception creating hesitation and eroding their confidence this transforms the battlefield of perception into a contested space where defenders no longer merely react but actively shape the attacker's psychology the cost of failing to counter psychological manipulation is immense because its effects are cumulative each successful manipulation reinforces vulnerabilities and weakens collective trust when individuals are deceived repeatedly they become cynical and disengaged when societies are manipulated repeatedly they fracture into polarized groups unable to cooperate when defenders are manipulated repeatedly they burn out and lose sharpness the attacker wins not by breaching systems but by breaking will thus psychological manipulation in cyber conflict is not a secondary tactic it is a primary strategy that strikes at the foundation of security which is trust to outsmart it defenders must recognize that the digital battlefield is as much about minds as about machines and that mastering human psychology is just as critical as mastering code

Turning Deception into Defense

While deception and psychological manipulation are weapons often wielded by attackers defenders can transform them into powerful defensive strategies deception in defense is about creating an environment where attackers are never sure whether they are succeeding where every step they take could be a trap and where time effort and resources are drained through uncertainty honeypots act as digital bait simulating vulnerable systems that attract attackers when engaged these systems reveal the tools techniques and tactics of adversaries without risking real assets defenders can then study this intelligence to refine defenses predict future moves and even attribute attacks to specific groups honey tokens go further by embedding false credentials documents or code snippets throughout the environment if an attacker attempts to use these decoys it signals compromise and provides defenders with early warning turning deception into defense requires creativity because it is not enough to replicate a simple decoy effective deception must mirror the real environment so closely that attackers cannot distinguish between genuine and fabricated systems automation enhances this process by constantly refreshing decoys ensuring attackers cannot map patterns over time deception is not limited to technology but extends to organizational behavior defenders can craft misleading signals about their security posture deliberately exposing false weaknesses while hiding true strengths this misdirection causes attackers to waste resources probing irrelevant areas and increases their exposure to detection another powerful use of deception is narrative control in the aftermath of a breach organizations can strategically release information that shapes the attacker's perception creating uncertainty about what data was stolen or whether the breach yielded any value this form of defensive deception denies attackers the psychological satisfaction of victory and undermines their confidence the ultimate goal of defensive deception is to flip the attacker's advantage against them since attackers traditionally benefit from surprise and initiative deception allows defenders to reclaim both by making the environment unpredictable deception also creates a psychological tax on attackers when every move could be a trick or a trap they hesitate their confidence erodes and their operational tempo slows in contrast defenders who master deception gain initiative time and intelligence they are no longer merely reacting but actively shaping the battlefield turning deception into defense therefore elevates cybersecurity from passive protection to active strategy it transforms defense from static walls into dynamic battlefields where attackers face uncertainty at every turn and where defenders can predict disrupt and outmaneuver even the most sophisticated adversaries.

CHAPTER 10

Cybersecurity as the Foundation of Digital Civilization

The digital world is no longer a parallel reality it is the very fabric upon which modern civilization is built the smooth operation of economies governments education systems healthcare infrastructures and even personal lives depends on the invisible currents of information flowing through networks yet the stronger our dependence on this fabric the greater the risks when it frays or is deliberately torn cybercrime is no longer an isolated activity conducted by fringe actors it has become a systemic challenge that endangers the survival of entire ecosystems the foundation of digital civilization rests on security because without it the entire architecture collapses trust which is the currency of digital interaction cannot exist in the absence of security when people fear that their transactions will be intercepted their identities stolen their communications spied upon or their governments manipulated by unseen hands they retreat from digital engagement the retreat may not be physical but it manifests as hesitation reduced innovation and a decline in social cohesion the entire promise of the digital revolution becomes compromised security therefore is not a luxury but the foundation upon which digital life itself stands and this recognition reshapes how societies must approach the concept of defense at the individual level cybersecurity is not merely about protecting devices but about protecting dignity because personal information today is not only data it is identity it is reputation it is the essence of who a person is in the digital realm to lose control of one's digital presence is to lose control of one's narrative in the modern world the ability to bank communicate learn and work is tied inseparably to digital access making security a form of empowerment and insecurity a form of disenfranchisement at the corporate level security has become synonymous with survival organizations that fail to protect their digital assets find themselves losing customers losing market position and in many cases losing the ability to operate entirely for corporations security is no longer an IT issue it is a boardroom priority a competitive differentiator and a brand promise customers today evaluate not only price and quality but also safety when choosing who to trust with their data at the governmental level cybersecurity underpins sovereignty because a state that cannot secure its digital frontiers cannot govern effectively power grids health services financial markets and defense systems all rely on secure networks adversaries who compromise these systems can paralyze nations without firing a single bullet the battlefield of sovereignty has shifted from land sea and air to cyberspace and governments that ignore this reality will find themselves vulnerable to digital conquest finally at the societal level cybersecurity is the glue that holds together modern digital civilization when public confidence in digital platforms weakens the social contract begins to unravel democracy is undermined by manipulated narratives economies are disrupted by cyberattacks and communities are fractured by disinformation the cost of insecurity is not only measured in financial terms but in the weakening of collective identity and trust in this sense cybersecurity must be redefined not as a technical concern but as the foundation upon which digital civilization rests it is the invisible infrastructure that sustains modern life and without it the very possibility of progress is compromised. Cybersecurity as the foundation of digital civilization is not a metaphor but a reality, because the modern world has reached a point where almost every function of human society relies on digital infrastructure. The flow of money, communication, education, health services, and even the execution of government authority are mediated by invisible systems of code and connection. Just as water sanitation became the unseen foundation of public health in previous centuries, cybersecurity has become the invisible infrastructure of modern life without which everything else collapses. When systems fail or are attacked, economies freeze, communication channels collapse, and trust evaporates, creating a vacuum that undermines not only convenience but survival. At its core, digital civilization is defined by interconnectedness and interdependence, yet these same qualities make it fragile. The same networks that allow collaboration across continents also provide pathways for hostile intrusions. The same platforms that connect billions for commerce and communication also enable the spread of disinformation and manipulation. The same tools that accelerate innovation also expand the attack surface for criminals and hostile states. The paradox is that the more advanced society becomes digitally, the more exposed it becomes to vulnerabilities, which means that security is not an afterthought but the bedrock upon which the digital era rests. Individuals who once lived their lives defined by geography now live their lives defined by networks. The phone in one's pocket is not only a tool for communication but a gateway to banking, identity, storage, navigation, and connection. A single breach of that device compromises not just private information but the ability to function fully in society. Thus, cybersecurity becomes synonymous with human dignity, because in a digital world the loss of data is the loss of autonomy, identity, and agency. Organizations function as the engines of progress, yet their survival now depends on their ability to preserve trust, and trust is inseparable from security. Consumers no longer ask only what a company sells but how safe it is to interact with that company. When corporations lose control of customer data, the damage is not only financial but reputational and often irreversible. Entire industries have collapsed because a single breach revealed that security was neglected. In the twenty first century, security is no longer a technical feature hidden deep within IT departments; it is a competitive differentiator and a brand promise. It is also the invisible contract between business and society, because businesses that handle personal information hold fragments of identity, and therefore fragments of life. The erosion of trust in these systems directly translates into erosion of trust in commerce itself. Governments, which historically maintained sovereignty by protecting borders, now face the challenge of protecting digital frontiers. A nation that cannot secure its data systems cannot claim true sovereignty. Power grids, health infrastructures, transport systems, military logistics, and democratic elections all depend on digital systems, and adversaries have already demonstrated that disrupting these systems can paralyze a nation without firing a bullet. The essence of power has shifted from territorial control to informational control, meaning cybersecurity has become the new frontier of sovereignty. The strength of a nation is measured not only by the size of its military or economy but by the resilience of its networks and the integrity of its digital command structures. Failure to secure these systems risks not only inconvenience but the collapse of governance itself. At the societal level, cybersecurity is the glue that sustains collective trust. Communities once built trust through face to face interaction but now rely on digital platforms where identities can be faked, narratives manipulated, and communities divided by coordinated disinformation. The weaponization of information has already shown its ability to destabilize societies, weaken democracies, and foster polarization. When people can no longer distinguish between truth and manipulation, the foundation of democracy weakens, and social cohesion deteriorates. Thus, cybersecurity is not simply about keeping criminals at bay; it is about preserving truth, integrity, and the possibility of shared reality. Without these elements, a society cannot function. The cost of failing to recognize cybersecurity as the foundation of digital civilization is immense, measured not only in financial losses but in the weakening of the social fabric, the collapse of confidence, and the erosion of future potential. The digital revolution promised efficiency, speed, and progress, but without security these promises to mutate into vulnerabilities, inefficiency, chaos, and regression. It becomes clear therefore that the sustainability of digital civilization depends on treating cybersecurity with the same seriousness that previous civilizations treated food supply, sanitation, and public safety. It is no longer enough to build digital systems with functionality alone in mind; security must be the first design principle. Just as no building can stand without a foundation, no digital structure can endure without security. To think of cybersecurity as secondary is to build skyscrapers on sand and hope that the storm never arrives. Yet storms always come, and civilizations endure only when their foundations are strong. The future of digital civilization rests on the recognition that every new innovation creates new opportunities for attack, and every expansion of connection increases the complexity of defense. Rather than resisting innovation, societies must integrate resilience into innovation, so that every step forward includes preparation for protection. Cybersecurity must not be reactive but proactive, it must anticipate rather than merely respond, and it must evolve as quickly as the threats it seeks to neutralize. This requires not only technology but governance, education, and culture. It requires international cooperation, because networks do not recognize borders, and an attack in one country can ripple instantly across the globe. Just as environmental sustainability became a shared global cause, cybersecurity must become a shared human priority, because the collapse of digital trust threatens the foundation of digital civilization everywhere. Ultimately, the recognition of cybersecurity as the foundation of digital civilization transforms how societies view progress. It is no longer enough to measure success by speed of connection or volume of data; it must be measured by the resilience of systems and the depth of trust. Progress without security is illusion, because it builds castles that crumble at the first sign of attack, but progress with security becomes durable, sustainable, and transformative. This shift in perspective demands action from every level. Individuals must recognize their role as custodians of personal and collective security. Corporations must embed security as part of their identity. Governments must frame security not only as a defense against adversaries but as an enabler of prosperity. In this way, cybersecurity ceases to be a technical niche and becomes the universal foundation of digital civilization upon which the future of humanity depends.

The Human Core of Digital Defense

While technology provides the tools to protect digital civilization the heart of defense lies in the human element machines may automate detection and algorithms may analyze vast flows of data but it is humans who design systems interpret signals and make strategic decisions yet paradoxically humans are also the weakest link in the chain most successful cyberattacks do not exploit complex technical flaws but simple human vulnerabilities phishing scams social engineering fraud and disinformation all succeed not because machines fail but because people are deceived manipulated or careless therefore the true strength of cybersecurity depends on addressing the human core of defense this requires a multidimensional approach that includes awareness education culture psychology and ethics awareness is the first line of defense because individuals who understand how attacks occur are less likely to fall victim organizations that train employees to recognize suspicious links to question unusual requests and to verify before acting create an environment where attackers find fewer openings yet awareness must be more than mechanical checklists it must be a cultural shift where individuals internalize the importance of vigilance the challenge is that awareness often fades over time when employees are trained once a year but face daily pressures of work convenience and speed they forget lessons learned effective awareness must therefore be continuous engaging and personalized so that security becomes second nature rather than an external imposition education goes deeper than awareness because it seeks not only to teach habits but to cultivate understanding individuals must learn not only what threats exist but why they work and how adversaries think this empowers them to anticipate manipulation rather than merely react to it when people understand the psychology of deception they become resilient against fear urgency and flattery which are the core weapons of cybercriminals education also strengthens defenders by creating a pipeline of professionals who can think critically innovate constantly and adapt to evolving threats without education societies risk running out of skilled defenders leaving the digital frontier exposed culture represents the collective dimension of the human core of defense when security is treated as the responsibility of a small technical team organizations remain fragile but when security becomes part of organizational culture embedded into daily operations it transforms into shared responsibility this cultural shift requires leadership commitment transparency in communication and reinforcement of values where security is recognized not as a hindrance but as an enabler of trust and long term success psychology plays a crucial role because humans are not rational machines but emotional beings attackers know this and exploit fear urgency and authority defenders must therefore cultivate psychological resilience both in individuals and in teams individuals must learn to pause reflect and question before reacting teams must learn to support one another to prevent fatigue burnout and cognitive overload which are the silent enemies of defense defenders who operate in an environment of recognition support and purpose remain sharp and motivated whereas those who operate under stress neglect and invisibility deteriorate over time ethics represents the moral dimension of the human core because the choices defenders make shape the future of digital civilization when companies are tempted to cut corners by hiding breaches when governments are tempted to exploit surveillance for control when individuals are tempted to misuse knowledge for personal gain the human core of defense is weakened cybersecurity without ethics becomes a double edged sword that may protect systems while undermining freedom the human element is therefore not merely a weakness to be corrected but a strength to be cultivated when individuals are empowered educated resilient and ethical they become the strongest defenders of digital life the human core of digital defense is not a barrier to progress it is the foundation upon which progress can safely be built. The human core of digital defense represents both the greatest vulnerability and the greatest strength in cybersecurity while the majority of breaches can be traced to human error negligence or manipulation it is also human creativity adaptability and resilience that ultimately determines the ability of societies organizations and individuals to defend themselves in the digital arena at the heart of this paradox lies the undeniable fact that technology alone cannot secure the world no matter how advanced algorithms become or how intelligent machines are trained to detect anomalies it is people who design systems people who implement controls people who respond to crises and people who must ultimately decide what is worth protecting and how it should be protected this means that the path to stronger cybersecurity is not only paved with better firewalls encryption or intrusion detection but with better informed better trained and more ethically guided human beings understanding the human core begins with recognizing the psychology of vulnerability cybercriminals have long known that people can be deceived manipulated and rushed into making mistakes social engineering is not a technical trick but a psychological weapon attackers exploit trust authority fear and urgency to trick individuals into revealing sensitive information or performing harmful actions when an employee receives a fraudulent email that appears to come from a superior asking for immediate transfer of funds the success of the attack does not depend on whether the system is patched but on whether the employee hesitates verifies and questions the unusual request when a citizen reads manipulated news on social media and shares it without critical evaluation the problem is not the platform's infrastructure but the individual's cognitive defenses which have been bypassed by emotional manipulation this highlights why defending the digital world requires strengthening human awareness and decision making as much as it requires strengthening code and protocols the cultivation of awareness cannot be shallow it must move beyond surface level reminders such as do not click suspicious links and evolve into a deep cultural consciousness where people view themselves as guardians of security in every interaction this culture of awareness must be embedded in daily routines in schools workplaces and homes just as hygiene became a cultural norm in protecting physical health cybersecurity hygiene must become a cultural norm in protecting digital health washing hands became second nature in the fight against disease in the same way verifying links encrypting communications and questioning unexpected requests must become second nature in the fight against cybercrime awareness however is only the beginning education provides the depth needed to transform individuals from passive users into active defenders when people understand not only what to avoid but why attacks work they develop intellectual resilience against deception teaching the mechanics of phishing the psychology of disinformation and the anatomy of ransomware empowers individuals to anticipate rather than merely react education must also evolve with the threat landscape just as adversaries innovate defenders must constantly refresh their knowledge societies that fail to integrate cybersecurity education into curricula at every level from primary school to professional training are cultivating generations that will be technologically advanced but defenseless in the face of manipulation beyond awareness and education lies culture the collective embodiment of values and practices when security is perceived as a burden imposed from above individuals comply reluctantly and often carelessly but when security is embedded in culture it becomes shared pride and responsibility organizations with strong security cultures celebrate vigilance reward responsible behavior and normalize transparency about risks this shifts the psychology of defense from fear of punishment to pride in contribution culture is reinforced by leadership that models secure behavior by peers who encourage one another and by systems that make secure choices the easiest choices in many ways culture acts as the immune system of digital defense because it responds collectively to individual vulnerabilities psychology further deepens the complexity of the human core because the battlefield of cybersecurity is not fought only in code but in minds humans are emotional beings attackers know this and use it to their advantage by crafting messages that exploit fear urgency or authority defenders must therefore build psychological resilience begins with the individual capacity to pause before reacting to reflect before complying and to question before trusting this capacity is not innate it must be cultivated through training repetition and reinforcement resilience also extends to teams which must guard against fatigue burnout and cognitive overload prolonged exposure to alerts incidents and crises weakens defenders not because they lack skill but because they lack rest recognition and support a team that feels invisible or undervalued becomes vulnerable to mistakes whereas a team that feels empowered appreciated and connected becomes sharper over time therefore psychological resilience is as important as technical competence the human core is also bound by ethics because cybersecurity decisions carry profound moral consequences governments corporations and individuals all face temptations to misuse their defensive capabilities surveillance can be abused in the name of protection breaches can be hidden in the name of reputation and knowledge can be weaponized in the name of profit when ethics erodes trust collapses and with it the foundation of digital defense cultivating ethical integrity is therefore essential it ensures that defenders not only protect systems but also uphold the values that give those systems legitimacy in the first place this ethical compass must be anchored in transparency accountability and responsibility so that security is not achieved at the expense of freedom fairness or human dignity yet the human core cannot be fully understood without also considering motivation defending the digital frontier is not merely a technical challenge it is an existential one individuals and organizations must feel that their actions matter that their vigilance is not a drop in the ocean but a vital contribution to collective safety when defenders see themselves as custodians of civilization's digital backbone their motivation becomes stronger than fatigue or fear motivation is fueled by recognition by leadership that values contribution by societies that honor defenders as protectors and by narratives that highlight the nobility of digital defense just as firefighters are celebrated for saving lives in the physical world defenders must be celebrated for saving trust in the digital one the future of cybersecurity depends on transforming the human core from weakness to strength this transformation requires investment at every level societies must invest in digital literacy to empower citizens organizations must invest in culture and resilience to empower employees governments must invest in ethics and governance to empower trust and individuals must invest in vigilance and self-discipline to empower themselves when the human core is neglected no system can remain secure but when the human core is cultivated no adversary can permanently weaken the digital foundation of civilization because every attempt at manipulation will be met by minds that are aware by teams that are resilient by cultures that are vigilant and by societies that are ethically anchored the human core of digital defense therefore is not an afterthought to technology it is the very essence of defense without which no firewall no encryption and no artificial intelligence can withstand the creativity and persistence of adversaries when humans are strong digital life is strong and when humans are weak digital life becomes fragile in this recognition lies both the challenge and the hope of the cybersecurity era

Envisioning a Resilient Digital Future

If cybersecurity is the foundation of digital civilization and if the human core is its heartbeat then the future must be envisioned as one of resilience is not the absence of failure but the capacity to recover quickly and emerge stronger after failure it recognizes that no defense is perfect and no system is invulnerable breaches will happen disinformation will spread and attacks will succeed yet resilience ensures that none of these events translates into collapse resilience begins with architecture designing systems with redundancy continuity and recovery in mind so that compromise does not cripple operations organizations that invest in resilient infrastructure backups and rapid response mechanisms find themselves able to withstand attacks with minimal disruption resilience also requires foresight which means anticipating not only today's threats but tomorrow's possibilities the evolution of quantum computing artificial intelligence and next generation networks will transform both attack and defense resilience demands that societies prepare for these transformations now rather than react later foresight also requires imagination because threats do not emerge in predictable patterns they arise from creativity adversaries are imaginative and defenders must be even more so resilience extends to governance because no single actor can secure the digital world alone international cooperation industry collaboration and cross sector alliances are essential cybercrime does not respect borders and disinformation campaigns do not stop at national boundaries resilience therefore must be global rooted in shared norms shared intelligence and shared responsibility societies that operate in silos will find themselves fragmented and vulnerable but those that build bridges of cooperation will find themselves stronger resilience also requires cultural depth it is not enough to design secure systems or train skilled defenders societies must cultivate cultures of vigilance curiosity and integrity where security is celebrated rather than resented where innovation and defense coexist rather than compete and where citizens view themselves not as passive consumers but as active participants in securing the digital commons resilience finally demands trust because without trust resilience has no anchor people must trust institutions governments and organizations to act transparently and responsibly and those institutions must earn that trust by prioritizing security openness and accountability in a world where trust is scarce every breach every manipulation every lie erodes collective strength but in a world where trust is protected resilience flourishes envisioning a resilient digital future therefore means more than surviving cybercrime it means building a civilization where security and trust reinforce one another to enable progress it means transforming fear into vigilance weakness into strength and vulnerability into opportunity the resilient future is not a utopia without attacks it is a future where attacks no longer define us because society has learned to absorb them without surrendering trust unity or vision it is a future where digital life becomes not a source of anxiety but a platform for growth creativity and collective strength the vision is not distant it begins with choices made today choices to prioritize security as the foundation to cultivate the human core as the heartbeat and to pursue resilience as the destiny of digital civilization.

www.ingramcontent.com/pod-product-compliance
Lightning Source LLC
LaVergne TN
LVHW101503200926
848483LV00001B/215